# THE
# BOOK OF JOHN
## (Not the one in the Bible)

*8-20-23*

*Enjoy !*

*John T. Long*

A MEMOIR OF ADDICTION AND RECOVERY
JOHN T. LONG

*I am responsible for what I see.   I choose the feelings I experience, and I decide upon the goal I would achieve.   And everything that seems to happen to me I ask for, and receive as I have asked.* -A Course in Miracles

# Table of Contents

# Dedication

To everyone who has and will enter my life that blesses me as my teacher. To the Supreme Guide Who is in each and every one of us that allows free will and choices. We are all Co-Creator's . . . what are you creating?

# Foreword

## By Jonny Enoch

Every once in a while, a great spiritual teacher comes along in an unlikely form. In the case of John T. Long, he was not born of a virgin in a manger preceded by three wise men following a star in the east. Instead, our story begins with a lawyer from Alabama who speaks with a Southern drawl and loves to smoke and swear.

He also possesses the rare gift of inner alchemy, which is the ability to transmute life's most difficult situations into greater understanding and soul growth. The sole reason why we are all here.

It is truly fitting for this literary masterpiece to be named after a book in the Bible due to the highly transformative nature of John's experiences. In much the same way Moses was given 10 commandments on the top of Mount Sinai, written in stone by the fiery finger of God, these divinely inspired pages are the revelations of a sincere and honest man who found love and gratitude after great tragedy and loss.

Perhaps one of the greatest misconceptions we have today is that spiritual books must be full of candy coated, sanctimonious stories devoid of the hard facts of life that make us all human.

We can see this firsthand when meandering down the aisles of the spirituality section at the local bookstore, as most "paperback suppositories" lose the reader in a maze of unrelatable, cryptic nonsense about get-rich-quick schemes, barely decipherable by the so-called gurus who wrote them. These "spiritual books" claim to have countless law of attraction theme (scheme) stories about their authors' seemingly delusional, self-absorbed, and illustrious saintly lives.

This is not the case with the Book of John; what you see is what you get. Actually, if we examine the lives of most spiritual teachers throughout history, we find that nearly all of them had a troubled past before completing their life's mission.

It has been said that we can learn the most from others by walking a mile in their shoes. Therefore, sometimes you have to stare through the serrated edges of a broken whiskey bottle or a half-imbibed whiskey glass sitting on the countertop of a bar in the middle of nowhere and pierce through the veil of pungent second-hand smoke to discover the meaning of life hidden within the lyrics to a familiar song playing on a dusty juke box full of quarters from across the room.

However, this sad music is the soundtrack to a magnificent story which is raw, uncut, and pure spirituality in its finest form. John demonstrates over and over again that even if we stray off course in life, we can always find our way home.

This book is undeniable proof that we are all chemists living out our experiences by experimenting in the laboratory of life, which is why the word experience is the same as "experiment" in French!

What makes John's sometimes disturbing, often hilarious, and wonderful tale so unique is his remarkable ability to use introspective-humor to transcend his pain and suffering and to laugh at himself.

Perhaps one of the greatest secrets to life is not to take ourselves so seriously and to accumulate a sense of humor. By seeing the gift of wisdom in everyday situations, even our pain and suffering can become our greatest teacher, allowing us to grow and evolve.

Keeping in mind, the pages ahead contain a journey into the bizarre and strange world of a spiritual dynamo, filled with profound wisdom, supernatural experiences, and laugh-out-loud situations that are sure to warm your heart in a way that warm milk, calcium bicarbonate, and antacids cannot relieve.

In fact, these true-life stories led the author into the heart of the Mysteries. In the spring of 2017, I had the great privilege of traveling with him to Egypt. It is there that I met this gentle giant and first encountered his sense of humor, kindness, and humility.

This book is a true pleasure to read from start to finish; not only is it written just how the author speaks, but its living words jump off the pages in mid-sentence, traveling up the optic nerve to two visual cortices through the rods and cones in your eyes, acting like nitrogen and hydrogen exploding in the pre-frontal cortex of the brain until you are left swimming in a maze of new and exciting realizations.

These are the strange, ostentatiously weird, and dark experiences of a man not afraid to face his inner demons and come back to talk about it. I hope this book finds a special place in the hearts and minds of every reader. And may you always remember that you are the author of your own story.

# Chapter One

## *Early Childhood Development*

"*Get out!*" she screams after a long night of arguing.

"I can't believe it! After all I've done for you. How can you do this to me?" I yell.

Both of my children are terribly sick and have a fever of 105. The next morning I amble over to the Amoco station across the street and call my parents to come and get us. It takes me all morning to reach them. I throw all of our stuff into two black plastic garbage bags. The small rack of clothes and my twenty-five inch Sanyo TV are put on the steps as we wait on our ride out of the junkyard.

As I sit outside of the phone booth, I look up in the sky and say, "Okay God, you can take it from here?"

Mother lay in the open casket while all my friends stream by. The morbid smell of formaldehyde mixed with the sweet fragrance of stale perfume, mothballs, lilies, lilacs and roses fill the air. Her hairdresser, Yvonne, did a good job on her makeup. She cherished the pearl earrings she's wearing that I gave her for Mother's Day some years back. She looks so peaceful. No more judgment. No more worry. I know she's not "gone." She'll always be with me in my heart. Her voice still speaks to me, her expressions always imprinted on my mind.

"John-NY," she'd say with a grimaced look on her face when I did anything she didn't approve of.

I never liked funerals. Father wanted an open casket. How tragic to have to stare at a lifeless, blood drained empty body. Everybody comes to look at the dead body and say how sorry they are. Who invented funerals anyway? Was it the owners of the funeral homes to see if they could make a dollar on a casket? Over the years it evolved into a ritual of the wake (renting the wake room), fancy caskets, rental of the backhoe, purchase of the "plot," the shovels, the tent . . . (Remember the days of the old west, simple pine box, dig a hole, dump them in?)

I want a Cajun band playing at my funeral. Death is the best thing that would ever happen to me. No more bills, no fear, no worry, and no taxes.

On the other hand, father takes it hard. His drinking escalates. I'm powerless over him.

Father works for General Electric as a major appliance salesman, an only child born from a half-blood Cherokee Indian mother and a Pullman Railroad father. Dishonesty of any sort doesn't enter his mind. His work ethic and bigotry are programmed into him. He tells me for the first time he's proud of me when I graduate from law school. I'm thirty-eight. Mother is a typical southern girl raised in Woodlawn, a suburb of Birmingham, perfectly honest (she thought) and in her eyes my older brother and I can do no right.

"You *have* to get a haircut." she'd tell me.

"You're *not* going to go out looking like *that* are you?"

"You've *got* to do something about those nose hairs."

"Look at that poor lady; she's all gums when she smiles."

"Ain't that a nigger?" she says starring at the TV.

"You ought to be ashamed of yourself," she'd say.

"We can't afford it. We don't have it." Lack was programmed into me early on.

If my brother and I would only act right, then they would be happy. What would the neighbors think? What would their friends think?

She doesn't believe in sex before marriage and is clueless about drugs. (Although she does admit to smoking corn silk with her two brothers and sister growing up). Rock music sounds like a foreign language to her. She keeps the house so clean you can eat off the floor and dust has no chance of accumulating anywhere. Dirty clothes are whisked away before they have a chance to hit the floor and float like a magic carpet to the washing machine. The cleaned-out pockets reveal an assortment of paraphernalia, seeds, marijuana, money, and rolling papers all of which belong to someone else. She tells me she wakes up during the night and wonders what it was she had worried about all day. Then she remembers and starts worrying herself back to sleep. She grew up on a small farm behind Connors Steel Mill on fifth Avenue South. Visiting her parents, Nanny and Big Daddy, reflects a step back to a time of self-sufficiency and simplicity. Vegetables, chickens, and donkeys fill the backyard. The basement is filled with old tools hanging by rusted nails and stained ropes embodying a small child's wonderland.

"Can I ride the donkey?" I ask Big Daddy as the roosters scurry around our feet.

"He'll roll over on you," he says with a chuckle as I mount the jackass fearlessly. A few steps and the half-horse starts to roll and death becomes very real to me that day as I lunge off his back and hit the dirt with a thump.

Uncle June has a habit of asking questions with a "huh" and whistles on all the s's at the end of most sentences. "How do you like school, huh?" "Where'sssss your mother?" Uncle Sam works for Johns Manville selling asphalt shingles and lives in Atlanta to pursue his "alternative" lifestyle. He develops lymphoma later on and passes when I'm in my twenties. Aunt Louise lives in Knoxville and her and my mother don't talk for twenty years over a resentment. One of my cousins wouldn't eat spaghetti unless it was left over and now I know why.

I make a clay model of the Sphinx in kindergarten. I don't remember how good it was, but I do recall having made it. I've always been fascinated with Egypt and the Pyramids. I have a girlfriend in elementary school and her name is Marie Murray. I think we met in kindergarten! I remember us laughing and kissing in the back seat of Mothers' car. I'm devastated when she moves away. I remember my mother picking us up from school one day with watery eyes and a contorted half smile on her face. I have never seen her cry. It's November twenty-second, nineteen sixty-three. President Kennedy has been assassinated. I was too young (six) to grasp the full meaning of what had happened *and* I was too busy trying to hold a lip lock on Marie.

I grow up in Crestwood at fifty-four zero one, Eleventh Avenue, South in Birmingham. I remember the Crestwood Shopping Center complete with a spinning barber pole, crew cuts, hairy floors, jacked up seats, and the buzzing of a thousand bees. (No one running with scissors here.) A time of real drug stores filled with stationary stools on silver poles capped in red leather. Real ice cream scooped into frosted mugs, root beer or coca cola floats. The smells of chemicals, Hallmark cards, and penny candy behind the glass seeping out the door. I get a free shock treatment at the twenty-nine cent gas station when I put my hand on a vise that was touching a shorted out fan. I couldn't move and father had to pull me off of it.

At six we move to Metairie, a suburb of New Orleans, and I slip cigarettes into my pockets from packs of Salem's left lying around the house. I ride my bicycle to the local seven-eleven and ask the clerk to use the bathroom where they store the cartons of Marlboro. I walk in the bathroom and stuff cartons down my pants. I fall in love with Cajun food, crawfish, and Mardi Gras while I observe the fun and laughter my parents seemingly enjoy while drinking. A canal runs behind our house where a variety of snakes, water moccasins, black racers, king snakes, minnows, and strange odors flow. I shoot the minnows with my BB gun. Rumor has it that a hurricane wiped out a snake farm located nearby and washed the snakes into the canal.

I think, *Why would anyone raise snakes?*

My friends and I ride behind the mosquito truck as it sprays DDT. I pretend I'm flying through the clouds! One time some friends of mine are in the backyard. My brother has left his Benjamin pump .22 caliber pellet gun on the picnic table. One of my friends jokes around and points it at Art, thinking it's not loaded. It is and the pellet strikes Art in the stomach. I run screaming in the house and get my Mother who immediately takes him to the hospital. It missed his main artery by a fraction. I see all the blood stains on the back seat where he lay.

We have a local bully in the neighborhood, and we're down at the canal shooting minnows. Standing on the viaduct that runs under the road, he comes up behind me and holds me over the water. The thought of going in that snake filled, toxic water makes my heart catapult into my throat out of my mouth and I begin to wiggle. As I fall toward the water reaching for anything that would prevent my certain death, I grab his ankle and we both hit the water running.

Another day a friend and I decide to skip school, go down to the levy, swim, and gather mussels. We stay all day, smoking rabbit tobacco and swimming in Lake Pontchartrain. Mother happens to be walking with her friends and notices my book bag near the trail. When I get home "from school" she confronts me. I think this is my first lie. (You can't lie to your mother).

I talk father into letting me cut the grass for the first time. He carefully explains to wear shoes and stay away from the blade. As I push the lawnmower past the wooden fence, I notice some purple berries growing up from the canal. I grab the bush to move them out of the way and the berries stain my fingers. I squish a handful and run to the house screaming as the liquid runs down my arm. Father turns into a white linen sheet and starts to run inside to call an ambulance.

I scream, *It's the berries*.

We move back to Birmingham in nineteen seventy and my parents buy a house in Mountain Brook on Westbury Road. Mountain Brook is the high society section of Birmingham where all the old money is. I never fit into the rich or athletic crowd, instead befriending the stoners, the free spirits, and the hippies. I grow my long blond hair to my shoulders and Big Daddy starts calling me "Shag." I play the chameleon and actor always worried about what other people think about me. Conform to society; go to school; get a college degree and I can accomplish anything I put my mind to Mother always says. Around this time I take my first drink. The owner of El Palacio Mexican restaurant lives a few houses down and we heard he stored wine in his garage. We sneak into his garage late one night and steal a case of Pussycat wine. Downstairs in our basement, my brother and I consume the shapely bottles into oblivion and vomit pink. I love the effect but the excruciating hangover sucks! I smoke my first joint shortly thereafter and don't have to deal with life anymore.

I never buy into the concepts of religion, hell or the devil. This God, Creator of Universes, all knowing, all seeing and omnipotent, the Creator of me, a divine eternal being Who is a part of Him, he knows when I will be born and when I will die. He knows my life, needs and desires. He knows if I will sin, what the sin is, when I will "repent" and be "saved." So in theory He knows all this before I am born. So, in theory, I am condemned to hell before I am born. But, "they" say, I have free will. That still does not preclude the fact that He *knows* what I am going to do! Makes sense to me . . .

I used to think I was gullible; however, a majority of the population believe in "saviors." Whether it be government, gurus, prophets, Jesus, Buddha, Mohammed, extraterrestrials, etcetera . . . *you* are a savior, a God, an eternal being in a human body. All the answers lie within *you*! The power is in *you*! These "saviors" were created to make you believe that you have to give your power away to "them." Many think "theirs" is the one true God incarnated in a human body (when in reality we are all Gods), miraculously born of a "virgin" birth, in a manger with cute little lambs and died for our so called "sins." (Which is a mistranslation from Aramaic meaning "miss the mark in archery.") I was born in love and I am eternal whether I'm in Heaven or Hell. The religions have created the greatest *story* ever told. So God created the earth and made Adam and Eve. (But, what about Genesis Chapter 1, Verse 26, God said, Let *us* make man in *our* image . . .). Then Eve was tempted by a snake, (poor women), which was really the Devil.   After a while, God decided to flood the world to destroy what he made, because it was a mistake. But, he told Noah to gather all 8.7 Million animals in one boat so they could re-populate the earth. People celebrate Jesus's birth by a fat man dressed in a red suit who flies around and gives presents to everyone.  Then in the spring when he supposedly died for three days and came back to life, (like a lot of other myths) a big rabbit comes and gives eggs to everyone. Oh, and he needs money, because you can't talk to this one true God unless you accept his "son" or else you go to hell where another guy in a red suit, horns, and a long tail pokes you with a pitchfork for eternity. Yeah, and He's omnipotent so he already knew all this, but he loves you unconditionally . . . Same thing goes for all the other religions that try to make you believe that something is promised you in the future. (Eternal life, 70 virgins, streets paved in gold, etcetera; an illusion). *You* are the creator of your life. The devil didn't make you do it, you did it. Good fortune comes from your alignment with the Source within *you*, not some imaginary figure bestowing you with gifts or tempting you with a snake.

Science, quantum physics, spiritual theories, and concepts prove that we live in a holographic universe. Our DNA is a self-organizing intelligent system that interacts with the holographic-morphogenic field by transference through mini wormholes. Our consciousness can affect and does affect our "reality" through thoughts, actions, and emotions through this quantum entanglement of all matter through the space-time continuum. "Dark Matter" is where everything exists. By focusing on and acting "as if," with emotion and actions, we call this "reality" into existence.

"What's the matter?" Your thoughts, emotions, and actions change your matter-that is, either good thoughts or bad thoughts change *you*, because you are the co-creator within the holographic-morphogenic field. Good matter or bad matter; healing/sickness; happy/sad.

Ever thought of someone and then you get a phone call from them or see them shortly after? Your future consciousness has connected with that reality and brought it into your "now" mind. We are all connected through this quantum field.

Moreover, racism is nothing more than self-hatred, superiority and fear directed at people, religions, organizations, and institutions. It's passed from parent to child, either consciously or unconsciously perpetuating this insane egoic belief that one race, institution, religion or culture is superior to another. Just watch the interaction of young children who play together without judgment.

Mother makes us go to church every Sunday at Canterbury United Methodist, but my brother and I go and sit in the balcony. We sneak off to the billiard room and shoot pool. We listen to the sermon broadcast on the speakers so we know about the topic if questioned.

In the meantime, the occult, transcendental meditation, Eastern mysticism, UFO's, reincarnation, and astral projection always keep my interest. I read *Many Lives, Many Masters* by Brian L. Weiss who writes about reincarnation and past life regression and *Strangers Among Us* by Ruth Montgomery who discusses walk-ins (walk-ins are higher spirits that "walk-in" to other people's bodies by soul agreement) and automatic handwriting. Area 51 and Roswell intrigue me. At twenty-five I have my first and only contact with UFOs. My first wife and I drive to Lake Martin to spend the night in a cabin a customer lets us use. I'm sober as a newborn infant. The air could be cut with a butter knife and as I stand on the dock tying bait on the fishing line, movement catches the corner of my eye. I look up across the lake and see two objects hovering over the lake approximately a hundred yards away, silhouetting against the hills. I'm close to Maxwell Air Force Base and assume they are helicopters on maneuvers.

I immediately think, *There's no sound*, and I begin yelling, "Laura, Laura!" I watch as the two saucer shaped crafts turn away from me. The red lights border the circular objects of interest and a red light blinks in the middle. They float four stories above the water. In an instant they're gone.

I discover sex for the first time when I'm thirteen. After that my motive is to find the dope, get the girl, get her drunk or high, and take advantage of the easy lay. I smoke pot with friends at "The Circle" (a dead-end street) while we watch for the Mountain Brook police cruisers that drive up frequently. We could tell by the headlights whether we need to stash and run or just wait and see who's coming to the party. I go to concerts, the Allman Brothers, Fleetwood Mac, Grateful Dead, Wishbone Ash, Emerson, Lake and Palmer or hang out at "The Corner" with my Jewish friends. This is my way of life. I play foosball and billiards in Woodlawn with friends. I discover whose parents are out of town so I can party.

I work at the Piggly Wiggly in Crestline when I'm sixteen. I stock groceries at night. When I get hungry I open a loaf of bread, take pieces out and seal the bag back up. I think, *What the shopper doesn't know won't hurt him.*

I walk into the cooler and open cans of crabmeat, take some out and put the lid back on. I take beer and put it in the freezer. When it gets cold, I "shot gun" the beer as fast I can. (Meaning, I punch a hole in the bottom and put it over my mouth while I pop the can open, allowing it to flow down my throat.).

I drive to school one morning after I shot gunned beers all night. A friend, Ramsey, and I swerve toward each other jokingly (like playing chicken) every time we see each other on the road. We cross the centerline and get back in our lane just before we meet. This time I see him coming towards me. I'm hung over and I swerve toward him. I wake to the sound of sirens. I can barely breathe as my ribs are cracked. My friend in the back seat breaks his back. My brother in the passenger seat hits his head and leaves a spot of hair in the windshield but is otherwise unharmed. A witness says he sees a dog run out in front of me. The seven people in Ramsey's Ford Bronco receive slight injuries. One of them talks to me in the hospital before the police get there and tells me of the witness who saw the dog. When the police come to interview me I tell them a dog ran out in front of me and I had swerved to miss him. (My brother tells the truth to my parents later).

The worst day of my life happens when a bunch of us go to an abandoned fire tower in Vandiver. We get stoned and climb up to the top and watch balloons drift over the mountaintops. A friend, Crawford, and I decide to walk down the mountain and meet the others on the road. The terrain is rocky and thick with trees and shrubs. We make our own path through the woods zigzagging down the steep mountain. Halfway down I feel a sting on my ankle. The yellow jackets cover my entire body. I can't see a stitch of my clothing. Crawford hits them off my back and kills a palm full with every strike. I start to run through the woods, flailing my arms, twisting, and shaking my body. After a few minutes, I feel most of them are off of me. I stop to catch my breath. I hear a rattle, look down, and see a six-foot rattlesnake coiled at my feet.

Crawford pushes me and screams, *"Run!"*

Later on that day another friend, Scott, and I drive around Lake Purdy. We come around a curve at the same time a dirt bike turns the corner. The bike strikes the passenger side of the car while I duck the body coming towards me. I jump out of the car and run over to him. He stands up and his left leg twists around like a corkscrew several

29

times and he hits the ground. I run to Highway one nineteen and flag a car down to call an ambulance. While we wait on the ambulance someone runs over and says a fisherman flipped his Jon-boat over in the lake and disappears. One ambulance arrives and takes the injured motorcycle rider off. The rescue squad search for the missing fisherman with grappling hooks dragging the lakebed. They snag him about an hour later. His bloated, sponged body turned blue. I'd never seen a dead body before. That night we eat at my parent's house during a lightning storm. The bolts strike the neighbor's roof and all around us while making loud electrical buzzes and sonic *booms*.

Another time we go to the quarry in Pelham to swim. I'm standing on the cliff waiting to jump in the water.

I hear a black man yelling, "Blue, Blue."

I run over to him and he says his friend, Blue, tries to swim across the quarry and disappeared. I see hands above the water line and we all jump in to try and rescue him. He's gone. I'm fortunate we don't find him. They snag him with grappling hooks a couple of hours later, his body turned heavenly blue.

My friend, Kevin, lives on the street next to mine. I learn to shoot pool at his house. His parents go out of town and leave him with the keys to their Lincoln Town car. A bunch of us pile into his car and we drive to Crestline Village. I sit in the passenger seat and a couple of people sit in the back seat.

As we approach the light about a mile from Old Leeds road and Montevallo, I turn around and say, "Y'all better put your seatbelts on; Kevin can't drive worth a shit."

A few seconds later Kevin turns to me and says, "Man, I'm gonna' get some pussy tonight!"

He turns back around just in time to see the car in front stopped at the light. He totals the Town Car. His parents never gave him the keys again.

I'm seventeen and my friend Chris and I are sitting back in the woods at a place we call "the rock." It's a rock outcropping where we all go to get high and drink.

We see two girls walking towards us and I look at Chris and say, "Look, a gift from heaven!"

Julie is my first "love." I become addicted to love. We date for the next year. One night we're hanging out in the neighborhood and I notice something different about her but I can't put my finger on it. I notice her and another male friend are kind of friendly. I confront her and she admits to fucking Jim in the dollhouse behind his parent's house. My brain is numb and my heart drops to my stomach. Jim always gets the women. He's good looking, rides a dirt bike, and is a know it all.

She writes in my high school annual "John, my love, I guess I will start from June eighteen, nineteen seventy-five and just keep going. I remember the first day I saw you was (sic) back at the rocks with Paige and you were with Chris. I didn't think much of you then but as I got to know you better the feeling changed very much. I know you will be going off to school soon and I know you will end up with the best of everything because the best deserves the best. Thorough (sic) our good times and our bad times, I feel we've learned a lot from each other. Never forget the times we made love and shared each other's love. Some of the best memories of my life were spent with you and I hope the feelings are mutual. No matter how much I lied to you or how bad I treated you, or even cheated on you, I still loved you. So it ends, you'll go your way and I'll go mine, hoping the dreams you've always had for your life will come true. Much Love Always, Julie."

She committed suicide some years later I'd heard.

One afternoon I come home from my senior high work-study job at Toy City (or toy shitty as we called it) and notice cars lined up along Westbury Road.

I approach my house and think, *Someone's having a party!*

My house appears at the top of the road and I see hundreds of people partying in the yard. My brother had previously announced my parents went out of town and he invited everyone over.

My parents asked my seventy-eight year old grandmother, Meme, to stay with us while they vacationed. She watched TV upstairs while everyone else drank, smoked pot, and took Quaaludes, Seconal, downstairs. Someone locked our dog, Bridgette, in the closet. The house is filled with pot smoke. I think it would be funny to give Meme a shotgun, (unknowingly to her, of course) where you put the joint in your mouth backwards and blow smoke into somebody else's mouth. My poor grandmother worships the ground my brother and I walk on. She sews real GI Joe clothes by hand to dress up my doll figures. (Is someone programming me for war?) When we stay with her in Tuscaloosa she makes the best whole-wheat muffins and "made from scratch" pound cake. My favorite is red velvet cake. She makes a little extra bowl of cake batter for me to eat. I love for her to tickle my arms ever so slightly to calm and relax me.

The manager of Toy City, Rick, likes to play tennis and leaves us at the store to run it. He buys a shit load of Evil Knievel toys for $16.95 and stocks them in the back room. At Christmas he sells them for $100.00 each. One day while the boss is gone, we decide to start ringing up the sales on a calculator telling the customers the register's broken. At the end of the day there are large stacks of money underneath the counter. We divide it up evenly between us. We all get fired, including Rick.

There's a curve on the road where I live that everybody calls dead man's curve. A motorcycle rider is killed when his bike runs through the curve down an embankment. They find his body a week later. My brother and I decide to go to the wreck site. We can see the broken branches and the trail where he'd left the road. My brother kicks a large rock and there's a clump of hair and scalp underneath it. The decaying flesh begins to diffuse the air. I'd smelled dead animals before, but this was like a mixture of a dead rat, burned flesh and rotten fish. It lingers on my nose hairs for days. Rotting human flesh, a smell that I will never forget. Like the smell of the beach, salty, suntan oil, relaxing, exotic and erotic. Or like the turkey roasting in the oven on Thanksgiving or Ham on Christmas and Easter.

Another time a friend, Wilson, and I go harvest a shit load of psilocybin mushrooms from a cow pasture in Shelby County. We take them back to his apartment and began the process of boiling them down to a liquid. The mushrooms eaten raw are pretty slimy so we cook them down and take them to a party over at Chase's parent's house. We pour the dark fiber laden concoction into a quart Tropicana orange juice jar along with those six ounce Dixie cups to the party. The mushroom juice is so concentrated and potent that I only need to drink about one-eighth of a cup to trip my brains out. I place the hallucinogen on top of a car in the driveway so everyone can share the ride. After everyone gets their dose, my brother takes the remaining liquid (amounting to three-quarters of the jar) and drinks it all! He sits in front of the fish tank all night staring at the fish and bobbing his head in circles. He's never been the same since.

Wilson and I go to Lake Martin on another occasion to fish. We fish all day and consume a bottle of bourbon. Wilson likes to drive fast in his Chevy Malibu. We speed down the country road at about seventy miles an hour. A stop sign suddenly appears in front of us and he slams on his brakes. We skid through the stop sign and come to a standstill in the middle of the intersection. We look to the left just in time to see a car slam into the left rear of the Malibu ejecting the spare tire 100 feet from the trunk, the car spinning around and landing in the gas station parking lot, occupants seemingly unharmed.

A witness pulls up and runs through the mist of antifreeze and asks us if we are hurt and says, "I saw death in the car when the spare tire flew out of the trunk. Are y'all sure you're okay?"

Wilson gets out of the car and calls his parents to come get us. About the time he hangs the phone up, the police show up. I put cigarette tobacco between my teeth and lips to hide the alcohol on my breath. They take Wilson to jail. They give me a breathalyzer test and I put the lip piece on the tobacco and blow. It fails to register and they release me to Wilson's parents when they arrive.

Crawford and I go over to Chip's house to investigate some horse tranquilizer he'd stolen from a vet's office. We decide to shoot it in our veins. We drive around and Chip is passed out in the back seat foaming at the mouth. We're scared of getting pulled over or him overdosing in the car so we drive to the dead end street that's the entrance to "the rocks." We take him out of the car and place him in the grass next to Will's house and leave.

I spend one summer with my childhood best friend, Bobby, as he convalesces from a motorcycle accident. We invent a game called Jamaican Crazy Eights. We play it just like regular Crazy Eights except a Jack skips a person; a two makes you draw two cards and tens reverse directions of play. Later on, when I attend the University of Alabama, I take this game to friends at the fraternity houses and everyone loves it. I never think much about it after I graduated until I play UNO years later and realize that's *our* game! A day late and a dollar short Mother always said.

# Chapter Two

## *Educated...*

I graduate from high school and enter the University of Alabama in the fall of nineteen seventy-five. My father knows the dean of admissions. He tries to talk me out of college because of my C-D average grades in high school. The keg parties, pot, and undisciplined behaviors prove him right. My friends elect me team captain of an intramural softball team and the loser buys the keg. The fraternity parties mean free beer and liquor and I take advantage of both. I get introduced to one of the sorority girls and ask her out on a date. Prior to the date, a fellow scholar and I share a bottle of Jose Cuervo exchanging shots with salt and lemons while drinking tequila sunrises. I go to the sorority house to fetch my date in my nineteen sixty-four neon blue Chevrolet Impala purchased that summer. I pick up a hitchhiker on University Blvd; drop him off, and we go by my dorm room to pick something up or try to have sex with her. (Can't remember which). I get out of my car and jump across the roof to open her door. I can't remember much after that except waking up the next day black eyed, beat up, and hung over. The six foot, four inch tall stranger I meet in the dorm shower informs me I tried to pick up his girlfriend the night before and he kicked my ass. The university places me on academic probation.

The second semester mirrored the first and they suspend me for a semester. That summer I work at Bethea National and break molds fresh out of the furnace. This factory in Pelham makes glass and metal connectors that hold the wires on telephone poles. The molds come off the factory line and I break the pieces apart with a sledgehammer so they can be assembled. The temperature on the line, where the guy who pours the molten steel into the molds, gets so hot that he develops a bubble in his blood. This causes him to have a heart attack! I quit that job and start UAB in the fall of nineteen seventy-six. I go back to Tuscaloosa for the spring semester of nineteen seventy-seven to continue my studies and drinking. I'm not able to keep up my academics that term and start working at Shoal Creek Country Club during the summer of nineteen seventy-seven doing golf course maintenance work. This is easy stoner's work.

Shoal Creek is a golfer's paradise. I start out repairing water lines for the sprinkler system. I shape and help build the greens and sand traps to get the course ready for the grand opening. They promote me to mow the greens and rake sand traps. I pull the lawnmower with a Cushman cart. On the way to the greens I see the deer play in the sand traps in the early morning hours. I see the turkeys strut across the fairways. I have four or five greens to mow. The immaculate and costly greens require careful attention. The self-propelled precision mower needs razor sharp blades and steady hands to keep the lines of the cut straight. It's nothing like mowing the front yard. I become proficient at keeping the mowed lines straight. The supervisor asks me to mow them for the grand opening, an honor really. Jack Nicklaus arrives for the grand opening. The owner, Hall Thompson, flies him in on a helicopter; it's a big event for Birmingham.

The next three years I alternate between working various other jobs doing carpentry work. I build decks and utility sheds for an apartment complex in Cahaba Heights. I do roofing work and attend the University of Alabama in Birmingham at night. I also attend Alabama in Tuscaloosa at various intervals. The smells of sulfur, fiery hot metal, treated wood, freshly mowed grass, dirt, and steaming tar remind me of days of hard labor, sweat, and sore muscles. The hard work motivates me to return to Tuscaloosa to finish college in the summer of nineteen eighty-one. During this time, (nineteen seventy-five through nineteen eighty-one) I have four DUI's, get arrested for breaking into a house and on another occasion get caught stealing a motorcycle.

"Put *that* in your pipe and smoke it," Mother always says.

I think, *It's just a case of being in the wrong places at the wrong time.*

In the spring of nineteen eighty-one my friend, Chris, and I decide to go drink at The Courtyard. I see her playing pinball. Her long blonde hair and perfect body sways to the rhythm and bells of the lit up machine. I swagger over to her mumbling and slurring my speech. I impress her enough to get introduced to her sister, Laura who believes that the way to a man's heart is not through the stomach, but a little lower. Her sexuality exudes from her pores. For me, a dream comes true. She says hello and I say I love you. We go on our first date to the Hollywood Country Club. The music drowns out her complaints of pain oozing from the drain of her ear infection.

She tells me she's a prostitute for the mafia and now wants out. They won't let her. She knows of a house on the Cahaba River where they keep drugs and money.

I think, "*Easy money*," as she, Chris, and I go there one night to rob them. We chicken out when we get close to the house because we hear people talking on the deck. She lives with her mother in Homewood off Valley Avenue and I drive over there with my Winchester 30/30 while her mother works. We fuck like rabbits. She receives phone calls from one of the mobsters she calls "Uncle" while I bask in the afterglow of sex. I'm curious and carefully lift the receiver up in the other room. I overhear a smoke-stained voice that tries to convince her they need her services and don't want her out. (Obviously good at what she does).

She moves into the Townhouse apartments on Eighth Avenue. Mother drops me off there on a daily basis and we attend classes together at UAB. We screw for hours before and after class! She gives me a blowjob in one of the bathrooms on campus. One afternoon during one of our long sex sessions, we're jolted by a knock on the door. The stranger at the door tells us that the employees at the Central Bank next door watch us through the window every day. They plan on filming us if we don't close the curtains!

One day she tells me, "I'm pregnant."

"Shit."

I drop her off at the women's abortion clinic (the one where a bomb went off a few years later) a few days later while I go see Chris to get high.

We take an art class together, introduction to drawing, during that spring. We decide to enter an art contest together. I spend weeks drawing and coloring a pastel of a bass jumping out of the water. She gets drunk one night and paints an oil picture measuring three by five inches. She completes it in an hour. It's a ghost standing behind a table with drapes bordering the frame.

*A fucking ghost?* I think.

I enter the contest with expectations of winning and lambast her pitiful, intoxicated painting. The Russian judge of the contest awards her first place; my rendering is considered worthless. A really good artist, she can draw human bodies that show muscles, hands, and faces in perfect detail.

I finally graduate in August of nineteen eighty-one with a BA in American Studies. I follow my mother's advice to earn a degree. It lands me a job at Western Supermarket bagging groceries. The American dream appears to be located in the early eighties oil boomtown of Houston, Texas, or Tex-*ass* as mother calls it. I ask my sex machine to go with me. She refuses unless we get married and so we do on February twelfth, nineteen eighty-two. We load up the brand new Datsun B310 my father buys me and hit the road kissing, laughing, and making out the whole way to New Orleans. We spend our honeymoon at Joan Sutton's house, a friend of mother's. We get pulled over in Lafayette for swerving all over the road. Drunken love. We decide to go to Bourbon Street that night. It's the start of Mardi Gras and our new life. We go to Pat O'Brien's and drink Hurricanes all night. We return to Joan's house and while consummating the marriage I pass out drunk with her still on top of me.

The delusions of grandeur always settle at the forefront of my thinking. The dreams of arriving in Houston to become a successful artist, corporate executive, or president of a high-powered company keep me motivated. With resume in hand I hit the streets of Houston and apply for jobs. I interview everywhere I find a lead. After three weeks I land a job at Entex Gas Company digging ditches and repairing gas lines.

*A minor inconvenience*, I think, *I can work my way up to become president of the company.*

Houston is filthy, dirty, and smells of oil. We move into a studio apartment in the southeastern part of town. Roaches crawl and bite us during the night while we sleep on the mattress on the floor. (I didn't know roaches could bite!). I dig ditches with Mexican Americans for six weeks. American General Fire and Casualty offer me a job as a claims adjuster at the same time Entex promotes me to the map room. I throw the shovel down and run to a desk job to work claims.

I drive to Birmingham on several occasions to secure my needed supply of marijuana. I find a local source that proves much easier than driving nine hours one way. I work as a claims adjuster and handle automobile accidents, storm damage, and worker's compensation claims. I have hour-long waits to check out of the grocery store. The three-hour rush to and from work and three million people proves quite the stress. The workload of four hundred claims is mentally exhausting. I easily handle the stress with continuous draws from my "one hitter" marijuana pipe in the bathroom. Migraines, cluster headaches, and severe gastroenteritis are the results of a small town boy, culture shocked.

We move from the roach infested apartment to a nice apartment on Westheimer Road, a main thoroughfare not far from mid-town. I receive a raise. I'm making about twenty-six thousand dollars a year and they give me a company car. Laura gets a job as an insurance clerk. We arrange to have the car that my Father bought me when I graduated from college, stolen. We needed money to pay off the loan we got to come here. I flirt with every cute woman I meet. One time I pick up a woman at a bar in Galveston and we fuck behind some apartment complex off the interstate.

I remember when Hurricane Alicia came through Houston. Laura's brother, Powell, comes for a visit and we smoke pot underneath a balcony while we wait on the storm to approach. The winds clock ninety miles an hour and we stand out in the wind and feel the wind pelt the rain against our face. The transformers start to blow up all around us and emit an eerie blue flame and white smoke. The rain blows sideways from east to west, begins to stop and the sky clears. The eye of the hurricane is directly over us. The wind comes to a standstill. Then the wind and rain begins to blow from the complete opposite direction accelerating back to ninety miles an hour west to east. We hoped to see a tornado but one never shows up.

We stay in Houston another year and then move farther from town to Katy, Texas where my oldest son, John, Jr. is born on August sixteenth, nineteen eighty-five. I'm standing in the delivery room watching as they pull my son's head out of the incision in Laura's stomach. I almost fall over as I see the squished head of the Monster from the Black Lagoon pop out.

I think, *All the drugs I used have damaged my chromosomes to create this monster child.*

After they clean him up and he pisses on the doctor, he's perfect. I thank God.

A position opens in Bryan, Texas, a laid back town adjoining College Station, home of the Aggies. The office window of the building where I work overlooks a small creek and wooded area. I bury the stress of the concrete and steel of Houston. We move to an apartment overlooking fields and post oaks where herds of deer come to play. I buy apples and corn placing them out in the field to entice them. It's mesmerizing to watch the deer literally dance and play with each other. My Mexican-American coworker becomes my supplier of marijuana. I learn to play golf and he teaches me how to make fajitas.

A year later the oil boom starts to dry up along with the company I work for. They begin to lay people off and close the office. My boss, whom everybody calls "Doc," comes into the office one morning and tells me, "Pack up your desk and put it in the car." He takes me home screaming and cussing the whole way as the angry cancer in his lungs tries to escape. Neither one of us will return to American General. The company car is the only one we own. We have no money, as usual, so I call my father to help rent a U-Haul to pack up and move back to Birmingham. I figure if I'm going to look for another job, it might as well be back at home. Several days later, we pack and load the U-Haul when a special bulletin comes on the TV. We stop and watch the news in shock and disbelief as the space shuttle Challenger explodes into pieces on the screen.

# Chapter Three

## *Working Man*

Resumes, interviews, and four years of claims experience land me a job with Continental Insurance Company as resident claims adjuster in Montgomery. We rent a house in the Eastdale section. They give me a company car and pay thirty-two thousand a year. I can climb the corporate ladder with them and eventually reach the American Dream. Life as a claims adjuster is great! I work out of my home in the days before computers and cell phones. I receive new claims by phone or fax machine. I cover the middle part of the state traveling to Dothan on the south, Phoenix City on the east, Clanton to the north and Pine Hill to the west. This provides the perfect opportunity to be alone and get stoned. The people tend to be mostly "good ole boys" that treat me with respect because I write the settlement check. Vegetables, home cooked meals, and loaned vacation cabins are all extra perks of the job. To celebrate our move we decide to eat dinner at the Elite, a landmark restaurant in Montgomery. Stoned, drunk, and humble I get up from the meal and proceed to the bathroom. As I near the hallway I notice a man approaching me from ahead and directly in my path.

I step aside to allow him to pass mumbling, "Excuse me sir."

"Excuse me. Excuse me," I say as we dance side to side.

The woman seated at the table next to me says, "Sir, that's a mirror!"

I like to play golf, hunt, and fish. This provides me with an excuse to get drunk and stoned. I feel I can concentrate better on weed during these activities. Someone gives me a .380 pistol and I take it fishing to Lock No. 3 Park near Demopolis. I stand by the bank and notice a car pull in and go around the circle. I think nothing further until something tells me to turn around. I look and a man with three fingers is standing about six feet behind my right shoulder.

"Y'all catching anything?" I ask, ready to throw the fishing pole down and draw the life saving device from its holster.

"We didn't come down here to fish," he says while eying the goods he thought he would take.

"Oh?" I say pulling my shirt up and showing my armament. His eyes get big as saucers and he starts to walk backwards in his silent footsteps while he keeps his gaze on the gun.

We buy a house where I learn to grow tomatoes and pot. My youngest son Hoyt is born on February second, nineteen eighty-one. His Apgar scores test just below ten indicating his body functions are normal. With only one eye open for several months it appears he is not quite sure he's in the right place. We have a swing set and while he stands in the middle of the two-seater swing he can rock it back and forth with perfect coordination. When he's three I take him and Johnny camping at Lake Eufaula during the height of crappie season. We catch a bunch of crappie right off the bank. I cook some canned spaghetti to eat and I mix the fresh fish in with it. It sounds like shit, but the fresh fish mixed with the tomato sauce and meat taste well. Johnny catches frogs all night and comes back to the camp with a pillowcase full of them. There must have been about twenty or thirty frogs in there. I love my boys. Johnny is the apple of my mother's eye and Hoyt, too. But when I take Hoyt to visit my parents he sits by the window crying and waits for me to come back. Johnny has my features and his mother's personality and Hoyt has his mother's features and my personality. Strange how that works.

The house we move into on Princeton Road in the old Normandale section of Montgomery has a poltergeist. Our neighbor talks about a ghost she sees often in the neighborhood. She describes him as a little boy who wears a white t-shirt and overalls. He opens cabinets and closes doors in her house. Laura has seen him running down the street. One time while I work in my office in the front bedroom the outside faucet turns on. I jump up and run to the window. There's nothing there. I run outside and see no one, but the faucet is running full blast. On another occasion, we wake up one morning and one of my oil paintings lay on the floor next to the front door. Apparently the ghost took my painting off the wall and tried to carry it through the door!

Seminars, meetings, and trips out of town provide the means to get away, all expenses paid. I go to Chambersburg, Pennsylvania where the company provides lodging at a women's college. The women bring us notes with phone numbers while we eat in the cafeteria. I attend school during the day, drink and screw into the night. I return home and my left nut swells up to the size of a racket ball. I think the Pennsylvania pussy has contaminated me and Laura. I can't sleep. I can't look her in the eyes. I confess. I go to the doctor to get the needed penicillin. I'm diagnosed with epididymitis. Laura works as a secretary at a construction site where they are renovating Montgomery Mall. Laura goes and immediately screws a coworker.

I work a lot of storm and fire claims over the next several years and write estimates on damage to mobile homes and houses. A tornado strikes an area just south of Clanton. When I pull into the driveway I notice the insured's mobile home is slammed by the wind against a line of trees. It looks like it had exploded. The insured describes how he went inside his father in law's house next door to get a wine rack. Before he starts back to the mobile home, he looks out the window and sees the pine trees bend over and touch the ground.

I look at him and say, "That wine rack saved your life!"

On another claim a fire completely destroyed the interior of a mobile home. The intensity of the heat melted the walls. I look up on one of the walls that's half melted and a clock with the face of Elvis still ticks.

Off to Charlestown, South Carolina to work the devastation wrought by Hurricane Hugo. I listen to stories of tornadoes dipping up and down out of the clouds and I see where one hundred and sixty-five mph winds sandblasted the paint off houses. I pass ships and houses tossed haphazardly onto roads. I hear stories about homes filling with water as the insured climb into the attic while sharks swim below them. I vicariously live the storm stories as people describe their experiences, real and embellished. One insured relays a story of how he stands with his back against the door of his house for eight hours and successfully prevents the wind from blowing it open. My company pays for a nice three-bedroom condominium on Kiawah Island right on the golf course. I hit my eight-iron to the limb strewn fairway and green from my back patio lawn. Adjusters from all over the country converged.

We work claims all day, drink and smoke pot all night while writing up the estimates of damage. Sometimes we travel into town and eat at the local restaurants. Other times we cook at the condo. One night we buy shrimp right off the boat in Charleston. The shrimp boat caught the shrimp that day in the Gulf Stream that flows off the South Carolina coast. The turquoise shell of the shrimp gives the meat a sweet salty flavor. I cook prime rib on one of those tiny tabletop grills and another roommate cooks shrimp scampi. It was one of those all-time memorable meals where everything is just right, atmosphere, people, taste, sight, and sound are in perfect harmony.

My fellow coworkers ask, "So you're from Alabama?"

"Where's your pickup truck with the gun rack?"

"So y'all lynch black people on weekends, huh?" And they're serious.

I pull into an insured's driveway and park to inspect some damage. I inspect the damage to the exterior of the house when the African- American homeowner arrives. She sees my Alabama tag and her eyes lower and her voice crackles. I finish the generous estimate and she thanks me with water in her eyes. She thought I'd short her on the settlement because I was from Alabama. (and lynched black people on weekends). The stereotyped boy from Alabama has a lot of mind changing to do.

I work a claim in Summerville where numerous pine trees fell all over an insureds roof causing substantial damage. The roof is basically intact except the trees broke the ridge along the top of the roof and punched holes in the decking. The entire roof needs to be replaced. The garage next to the house is completely destroyed. I write the estimate and settle the claim. A few days later, President George H. W. Bush visits that same house.

On another claim I listen to an insured tell the story of how he sees his neighbor, a preacher, climb on top of his roof and rip the shingles off with his hands so he can get a new roof. He tells me how he stands at his sliding glass window and watches tornados dip up and down out of the clouds taking the tops off the pine trees in his back yard. I can clearly see the twisted and sheared pines cut in half from my rooftop vantage point. Anxious about whether or not I'm paying for a new roof (since there was no visible damage to it) he asks me if I see any damage.

"Sir, you stood at your window and watched tornados in your back yard. I think I'll pay for a new roof," I say looking down at him from the rooftop.

Allstate, State Farm and the "lesser" insurance companies argue over half-sheets of plywood, paying only for half of a roof and partial paint jobs while we pay whatever is more generous.

The end of my four-month "tour" dissolved stereotypes and everyone applauds me when I leave.

I arrive back in Montgomery and the idyllic marriage begins to deteriorate.

"Can you help me lift this?"

"My back is killing me."

"I've run out of pills, can you call the doctor?"

"The pharmacy?"

"Can you take me to the emergency room?" she says as she vomits and shits constantly. She stays fucked up all the time. I take care of the boys, cook, clean, and wash the clothes while she lies in a stupor all day watching TV. I can't wait to get stoned and leave for work every day.

One night I dream of a Chinese man who says, "I'd like to introduce you to your soul mate, Teresa."

We're standing next to each other like you do when you get married. The Chinese man is in front and facing us. I turn towards Teresa and see her face. I wake up that morning after the dream and explain the details to my awakening wife.

"But I thought *we* are soul mates," she says dejectedly, slinging the sheets off while reaching for the pill bottle next to the bed.

I'd worked for Continental for almost four years now and I want to see if I can get a promotion, so I ask my supervisor what I need to do.

"Why don't you take a few classes at Jones School of Law?" he says.

I think, *Hell, I might as well go full time and become a lawyer and make a lot of money*!

The delusions of grandeur continue . . . getting a student loan and having the company pay for it seems like the lawyerly thing to do. I take the LSAT and apply at Jones School of Law. I pass the test and they accept me into law school. I work full time and go to class three times a week for three hours a night. I get in a routine and school becomes easier as the semester progresses. After class we go out and drink. I come home to massive piles of laundry, dishes, and empty pill bottles. I cling on the edge of the bed hoping I won't touch the beast; one wrong move and I will fall to my death. She goes to rehab at Bradford and comes home after three weeks, happy, joyous, and free.

One night we have an argument and I threaten to leave. She takes my car keys and throws them out into the yard.

I scream, "I don't love you anymore!"

We go to talk in the bedroom. I tell her I want a divorce and she says, "Bring the children in and tell them." They are eight and four.

"Can you get me a glass of water?"

"Get your own fucking water!"

Her family is in disbelief that I stayed with her for twelve years and my family is in relief I have finally come to my senses. We file for divorce in nineteen ninety-three and agree to the terms for three hundred and fifty dollars attorney fee. I move my stuff into the mother in law addition of our house for "the sake of the children." She acts suspicious since her return from rehab and I listen to her secret phone calls outside her bedroom window at night. I hear flirty talk and laughter. When I confront her about it she admits to an affair with a twenty year old boy she met at rehab. I move to a small one bedroom apartment next to Montgomery Mall. I take what little furniture I can pack into a borrowed pick-up and tell her she can have the house, the riding lawnmower and the furniture. "You really know how to pick 'em, son," Mother always says.

I'm soon laid off from Continental so I start volunteer work at the Supreme Court building in downtown Montgomery. I meet Shannon at the Ramada Inn bar and we move in together and get engaged. I continue going to Jones and search for work during the day. Shannon starts getting phone calls and leaves the room or goes outside to talk. I confront her and she admits to having sex with one of her co-workers. Shit! I leave Montgomery and move into a one-room cabin at Cherokee Beach Campground in Bessemer. I find a job and start work at Goldome Credit Corp. doing foreclosures. The cabin's sixty-five dollars per week and seems prudent. The journey from the cabin to the shower in freezing weather proves idiotic. Leaving my two sons rips my heart out.

I apply at a law firm located in the Galleria. I go to interview for the job with the owner. With twelve years of investigating and negotiating experience as a claims adjuster I convince him that I can make him a lot of money. I continue to work at Goldome and hope and pray I get the job.

I'm sitting in my cubicle a few days later. An African-American female co-worker whom I do not know comes over and hands me a yellow sticky note that says:

"John-God said to tell you that he has heard your cries and that your prayers have been answered. He has opened the door for you for this job. The job is yours. You shall receive a call or through the phone. (sic) You will be told that you have the job. God said to spend more time with Him and that He loves you."

Several days later, the owner of the law firm calls me and says, "You have the job. When can you start?"

He hires me as a claims manager with the firm. I settle injury cases during the day and travel to Montgomery for classes three nights a week. I still live in the cabin when I'm awakened in the middle of the night with fire ants crawling on me and biting me.

I cry out to God, "Please get me out of here!"

Shortly after, the owner of the firm offers me a place to live on his farm in Montevallo in an apartment located over his horse stable. The constant smell of horse mixed with straw, fumigate me to sleep nightly with dreams of becoming a high-powered lawyer. "You can do anything you put your mind to," Mother always says.

Visitations with the children become a little easier physically as their mother moves closer to Fairfield, then Valley Avenue and finally Raleigh Villas in Homewood. They become harder mentally when I go to pick them up for visitation. They wander in, out of, and through the dirty laundry, scattered toys, and dishes caked with food in the sink, while their mother lies passed out in a stupor on the sofa. I get custody of them in nineteen ninety-four with help from one of the lawyers who work at the firm. I move to an apartment in Centerpoint. I take them to school, fix Johnny French toast and Hoyt cheese omelets every morning. I cook meals every night.

An aunt of one of the secretaries who works in the office tripped and fell at H & R Block and broke her wrist. My job is to gather the medical bills and records and submit them to the insurance company to settle the claim. The aunt suffers from brain cancer and is close to death. The owner asks me to research the legal issue of whether or not a claim for damages is extinguished upon death. I do the research and discover if a lawsuit is not filed against H & R Block before she dies, there is no claim. I advise the owner of this and he tells me to hurry up and settle the claim. The aunt dies. I'm instructed to settle the claim anyway and I do for thirty thousand dollars. The owner is always yelling at someone in the office. He's an asshole, but he's got a good heart. One of the attorneys reports him to the Bar. They investigate and send someone to question me. I tell them I didn't know. I'm white as a ghost when I leave the conference room and everyone asks me if I am okay. I'm not a good liar and Mother would always say, "It's written all over your face." The Bar makes the owner give the money back and slaps him on the wrist. Later I hear he's diagnosed with testicular cancer.

# Chapter Four

## *Not Again*

The summer of nineteen ninety-five I receive notice of my twenty- year high school reunion. The dreams of possible romance fill my loins. The steering committee plans the event to occur at the Birmingham Country Club. I arrive at the club fairly confident of who I'm trying to be. I see Susan from across the room; she looks like a princess, five foot six with shoulder-length dark brown curly hair. Her complexion radiates a light brown Italian glow. Her face is smooth and silky with a nose perfectly sculpted, apart from a slight imperfection at the septum. Her dark topaz eyes reflect little sparkles of light and her paper bright smile tickles my joy. The alcohol provides the needed courage and I start joking with her about the milkshake she's drinking. (A White Russian). At the end of the night the princess gives me her phone number. She kisses me on the cheek as her carriage whisks her away into the night.

"We'll be married within six months," I boldly confide to my friends as they laugh with skepticism.

Susan works as a secretary for Emanuel Counseling center with Rick Ousley, the minister of The Church at Brookhills. Susan loves Rick and would've been devastated by the affair he admitted to several years later. She works as a CASA (court appointed special advocate) worker for Jefferson County Juvenile courts. She also takes in severely emotionally and mentally disturbed children from Glenwood Mental Health. She feeds and takes care of them for days at a time in her apartment. I admire her for that. Her two beautiful daughters and a son reside with their father. She suffers several bouts of asthma and gets raped while we date that fall; however, I think nothing of the asthma or the rape. I'm determined to marry her and live happily ever after.

I'm in my final semester of law school when Susan decides to move from the apartment where she'd been raped. I go to the U-Haul store to rent a truck; the clerk insists that I purchase insurance. I refuse and the clerk goes out to the truck and marks all the dents on the rental contract. I check "decline insurance" on the form. I return the truck the next day and they charge me insurance.

I'm furious and write the Attorney General's office and the president of U-Haul at their home office. I attach proof that I refused to pay for insurance coverage. A few weeks later I receive several ten-dollar checks from U-Hauls all over the country. The home office writes me an apology saying they are changing their policy and will no longer force mandatory insurance. I think, *One person really can make a difference*! Thanksgiving night we make love for the first time. I ask her to marry me shortly thereafter.

We plan the wedding for February third, nineteen ninety-six at Canterbury Church in Mountain Brook. Each of our previous marriages had been sealed at the courthouse and we both want a church wedding. I graduate from law school and plan to take the bar exam at the end of the month. We rent a big house on Shades Crest Road in Vestavia on a steep hill that leads down to Rocky Ridge Road. Just prior to the wedding she begins to receive phone calls and acts very disturbed. One time I pick up on the other line and overhear a man with a smoke-stained scratchy voice coming from the depths of hell. The sound gives me goose bumps and makes the hairs on the back of my neck stand up, sending shivers through my whole body. My fear can't decipher what he is saying. I confront her about this and she claims that her parents would take her to a cave in Clanton when she was a little girl. The devil worshipers performed Satanic rituals on her and inserted knives into her vagina. The man who raped her the previous autumn was one of those people. The scars inside of her vagina make her story believable.

I think, *Too late to back out now*, as I shove the memory deep inside me. (No pun intended)

The wedding plans, details, and excitement are quashed by a phone call from the church advising us that the approaching ice storm necessitates the cancellation of our union. It's the first time in the one hundred year history of Canterbury Church they had ever cancelled a wedding. As the snow and ice began to penetrate the atmosphere with great wrath, we hurry to make plans to seal our fate at my parent's house. The roads start to become impassable as we leave our house. I let Susan (Sue Sue as her family and friends call her) go first and she barely makes it down to the bottom of the ice laden road. I turn around to go a different route as I wave at her to go ahead and we'd meet at my parents. When it snows in Birmingham people stop their car and leave it where it sits, whether on the highway or interstate. I dodge cars all the way to my parents' house.

We all gather at my parent's and wait on the minister to arrive. The phone rings. The preacher's stuck on Highway two-eighty and can't move his car. I convince the neighbor to go pick him up in his four-wheel drive Jeep. We hurriedly get married and celebrate my son's sixth birthday. We make it back home just before the roads are completely impassable.

We consummate the marriage that night in the new marital residence while the snow and sleet pound the roof. The next morning we awake to the first day as a married couple. Johnny, Hoyt, Faith, and the pet Shih Tzu all embark on a new adventure. We'd stocked up on milk, bread, Budweiser, and pot. We all begin to play in the freshly laid snow and ice. The fresh and crisp air illuminates the sparkling trees and their ice-laden branches. We all stand in the front yard and watch the seemingly brakeless cars slide down the hill. They crash ever so slightly into other cars abandoned long before them. I laugh so hard it makes my stomach hurt while rolling on the ground.

I find an old wooden sled with red steel rails on the sides, wooden slats to lie on, and a wood T shaped steering wheel that actually works. I sled down Shades Crest Road at seventy miles an hour, it seems. I'm able to stop only by steering forcefully up a side street. The boys get on my back and we have to roll off the old sled to completely stop it. It's exhilarating! Susan comes out of the house a little later and wants to join in the fun. She seats herself on a round plastic sled with handles on the side, belonging to one of the neighbors. She flies down the driveway uncontrollably and gets airborne over the neighbor's retaining wall. She lands squarely on her ass and fractures her hip. Unable to walk, I carry her into the house, lay her on the bed, call an ambulance, and continue my play in the snow. Eight hours later, the ambulance arrives and whisks her to Brookwood Hospital where she spends the next two weeks in recovery.

A few months later, *The Birmingham News*, May twenty-fourth, nineteen ninety-six, Scribblers section read:

"Never Too Late."

"Though Mother Nature did her best to spoil their special day, Johnny Long and Susan Cole got married anyway! This is the way an invitation to an after-wedding party dinner began.

The dinner took place belatedly on May 4 after a wedding in February. The wedding had been planned for February 3 at Canterbury United Methodist Church and had the distinction of being the first wedding ever canceled. Undeterred, the couple was married at Johnny's home by Rick Owen who came by way of four-wheel drive. The reception dinner fell victim to the ice storm."

I take the bar exam on February twenty-eighth through the thirtieth, nineteen ninety-six. It takes two months before the results are posted in the local courthouse. I stay positive about the results and never doubt that I did well. I need a score of one twenty-eight to pass. My score is one twenty-nine.

Mother says, "You don't need to tell anybody that."

My first trial is a case that involves a contractor who steps through a roof while conducting repairs. He falls through the skylight and breaks his ankle. The owner of the firm gives me the file on the Friday before the case is set for trial on Monday. It's a jury trial and we're the first case out. I open the file and there's nothing in it but the client interview. No medical records. There is nothing to prove damages. I work all weekend preparing. We pick a jury on Monday and try the case.

At lunch the defense lawyer tells me, "There's no way you're going to win this case."

I'm pissed and go write one of my best closing arguments in the chapel of a nearby church. We get back and I close the case. The jury's out for about an hour and comes back in our favor. I ask the jury foreman why they decided in our favor and he tells me they liked my client.

The law business is great! I'm getting lots of business and making money. Former clients refer me more clients. I'm down to earth and tell them the truth rather than taking their money and giving false hope. On the other hand, Susan is getting worse.

"I can't breathe," she says as she fumbles hurriedly for her inhaler.

"My throat hurts."

"I don't know what this pain is."

"I need to call the doctor, the nurse, the pharmacy, the ambulance."

"Can you pick up my prescription on the way home?"

"Can you take me to the emergency room?"

"Call the children; I'm not going to make it this time."

"Don't let them keep me alive artificially," she says psycho- somatically.

My frayed nerves are calmed only by a steady intake of alcohol and pot. Her face and body puff up like a blowfish from all the prednisone she takes, and a severe asthma attack the following summer of nineteen ninety-seven lands her in the hospital on a breathing machine. When she comes out of the coma she can't move any part of her body except her lips. Neurologists, psychiatrists, and specialists of all persuasions can find no cause for the imagined paralysis. They transfer her to Lakeshore rehabilitation. The paralysis baffles everyone. I convince the nurses to allow a conjugal visit.

She gets released from Lakeshore unable to walk so we move from the Shades Crest location because her wheelchair can't make it up the steps. We find a house not too far away at seventeen-fifty

Vestaview Lane. I build a handicap ramp so she has easy access to the back entrance. We trade our car and money for a handicap van complete with hydraulic lift and driving apparatus. Our bedroom turns into a hospital room. She lives, talks, and breathes asthma. All her conversations are about her sickness. She goes to the doctor, to the drug store, to the hospital, and to the emergency room weekly. Doctors, nurses, and home health aides are her only world, competing for the attention and affection I long for. She helps the children with their homework, cooks dinner, and cleans the house, sweeps and mops while driving in her wheelchair. While she's in the hospital, it's my duty to take care of the job, the house, and the children. During these times I learn to meditate for long periods of time lying in the bathtub, ears under the water, with soft music playing, and scents of lavender in the air. I sink into the calm silent water and concentrate on my chakras. I envision them expanding and contracting like a balloon. I'm led to the bookstore. I walk straight to the new age section, don't think or look, and pick up and buy *Conversations With God* by Neale Donald Walsh. Neale mostly confirms my beliefs in God, the universe, hell and the devil.

Her preconditioned, programmed Christian beliefs make her tell me constantly, "You're going to hell if you don't accept Jesus Christ as your savior."

"There is no hell," I say with confidence.

A lot of people make fun of or judge my beliefs, ideas, and sometimes
my actions because I go against the mainstream "stories." However, I
know this will shock you, there are tens of millions of like-minded
person's who think just like me! Scary, isn't it? I tend to look at facts,
logic and reason and my beliefs change upon new information, although
truth, honesty, and integrity in me never change.

No matter what anybody says, *everyone* is right, according to
*them*! What is "right" for me is based on *my* lifetime of
programming, conditioning, research, influence, experience, etc. Same
for each individual. There is no right or wrong, except for your right or
wrong according to you. So stop trying to tell people your right is better
or truer than theirs!

We argue one night after I purchased a watch I had been paying on layaway. She tells me that I shouldn't spend money without discussing it with her first.

I slam my fist down on the counter and yell, "I'll spend *my* money on whatever the fuck I want," as I storm out of the house and head to Jitterbugs lounge for a drink. The tornado warnings sound out everywhere, but I need to show her who's boss by getting drunk! The "category five" tornado touches down in Oak Grove that night, about five miles from where I'm drinking. The next day I gather clothes in the handicap van to take to the devastated area. I want to see the damage, not help anybody, really. I manage to convince the police to let me in, and I survey the damage from a strategic location that overlooks the small town of Oak Grove. The wind has literally broom-swept the entire house off the concrete slab foundation where I stand. Not even a crumb of dirt or twig remains. The next day, President George W. Bush stood on that same foundation and surveyed the damage!

I think, *Are these Presidents following greatness?*

The bathroom with the tub is located off the main hall of our house. Susan drives her wheelchair up to the bathroom door. She pulls herself up to the door while holding on to the doorknob, struggling. I'm curious to discover how she leaves her wheelchair by the door and takes the required eight to ten steps to the bathtub. One night I peep through the bathroom window and see her towel drop, walking effortlessly without strain or support, directly to the tub. Shocked and bewildered I confront her.

"Impossible."

"I'm paralyzed and can't walk."

"I couldn't have."

"I held onto the counter," she says imploringly.

"She can't walk. She's paralyzed," the physical therapist says suspiciously with tight lips and squinty eyes. Maybe I was hallucinating, as I take continuous hits off my pipe and bury more memories deep into the recesses of my mind.

The house we live in is sold so we move, again. She finds a ground level apartment at Cross Creek in Hoover. The asthma attacks continue to get worse. We have a small bedroom in the rear of the apartment that slowly begins to fill with hospital supplies, medicines, breathing machines and devices, medical waste dispensers, suction devices, a pharmacy, containers, oxygen mask, oxygen tubes, and oxygen tanks. Our bed transforms into a hospital bed complete with controls to move it up and down, recline and decline. The home health nurse visits become more frequent, administering shots, breathing treatments, and physical therapy. The gurgling, hissing of the breathing machine constantly echoes in the background. My meditations become longer.

Friday in September of nineteen ninety-eight, the final asthma attack hits her hard and the ambulance rushes her the hospital, for the umpteenth time. I stay with her all-day and late into the night and she tells me, "Call the children and tell them I'm not going to make it this time." Again.

I tell her "I love you" for the last time. The asthma worsens and they induce her into an anesthetic propofol coma.

Seeking escape, I go to back to the apartment. I take the phone off the hook and go out to get drunk at Senior Frogs while the children sleep in their rooms. I arrive back at the apartment in a drunken stupor. I put the phone back on the hook as the heart-piercing ring shatters the early morning silence. The nurse on the other end has been trying to reach me all night. Susan's heart stopped for an hour soon after I left her bedside. No oxygen to the brain is my immediate thought. I know she's sedated and there's nothing I can do. I cry myself to sleep.

I go to the hospital before work the following Monday, nerves long ago shot. Her doctor calls on the way and says, "We did an EEG and there are no signs of any brain activity."

I call her mother and her daughters and we gather in a white, stale, lifeless conference room of the ICU. The click, forced-pump machine breath, click, pump machine breath, click, machine breath, click, breath of the life giving device echoes in the background. Her mother and I make the decision to unplug the horrific noise tapping against my skull. The family gathers around the bedside and the nurse turns the switch to *off* as I stare at the heart monitor. Beep, sixty, beep, fifty, beep, I can't take it and run outside, light a cigarette and take a few strong pulls. I run back to her bedside, beep, twenty, and my heart and mind scream in pain; hers screams for life. The monitor hits zero and flat lines. The piercing steady beeeeeeeep shoots through my heart like an arrow. I collapse on her in tears. No more pain. No more suffering my baby.

# Chapter Five

## *The Beginning of the End*

The funeral: type of casket, metal or wood; lined or unlined; silver or gold; lilies or roses; time; date; open or closed. Her uncle offers to pay for the funeral and I accept. My parents are out of the country on vacation in Provence, France. I finally get in touch with them and make the arrangements for the burial on the family plot at Elmwood cemetery. I place a fresh rose on her swollen body. The tombstone reads "My Baby."

"She really loved you John. She told me she never loved anybody like she did you," her mother says.

A card Susan had given me years before reads: "You have truly changed my life. Thanks for coming into my life bringing love and happiness, I love you more than you will ever you (sic). I love you, Susan."

I tell myself she is better off where she is. Does "Heaven" exist? What's it like? Streets paved in gold? (As Mother believed) Many mansions (dimensions?) Seventy virgins? Woo hoo! The existential quest . . .

According to Nassim Haramein, William Brown and many others, our DNA is a self-organizing intelligent system that interacts with this field by transference through mini-wormholes. Our consciousness can affect and does affect our "reality" through our thoughts, actions, and emotions through this quantum entanglement of all matter through the space-time continuum. We are all Gods in these biological unit bodies, experiencing "life" in all its many forms. We are all part of the "One" mind experiencing Itself through us. I like to think of the movie, *The Avatar;* where our "real selves" exist in this other dimension directing it's thoughts into these human bodies, experiencing life. Why do you think it was so popular?

What's the matter? Lighten up! History, His Story is being experienced through *you*! Again, your thoughts, emotions, and actions change your matter. Either good thoughts or bad thoughts change *you* because you are the Co-Creator with this intelligence. It's your choice (free will) to be or do anything you want to create. It doesn't matter! Have you ever thought of someone and then you get a phone call or see them shortly after and they say, "I was just thinking about you!" That's because you have connected with them through this field and brought them into your "now" mind. Everyone and everything is connected through this quantum field. It doesn't exist without you being the observer of it.

You can't change Who you really are, a spiritual being, a God in a biological unit, co-creating with this infinite intelligence. What you can change is who you think you are. This totally explains what happened to Susan. She lived, spoke, breathed, and talked about her sickness and it killed her. She thought it into existence.

I shake my head. Her best friend brings a box of papers Susan had left when they used to live together. I come across a piece of paper that says, "I love you."

*Why did I leave her that night?*
*If only I had treated her better.*
*I should have called the children.*
*I should have called her mother.*
*I could have ...*, I think as the pain in my heart and incessant chattering in my mind can be cured only by numbness. Pot doesn't work anymore. Drinking only makes the pain and sadness worse. Her daughter, Faith, has a boyfriend that happens to deal in the needed solution to my problems, cocaine. Not only did it anesthetize my nose and throat, but also my mind and feelings. The clinical, laboratory smell of the bump of cocaine at

once transforms me! I am all-powerful, invincible. No more sadness, no more pain. I can drink all night, too. I go back to the apartment and throw all the sick paraphernalia into the dumpster.

A flurry of one-night stands, girlfriends and cocaine help me forget. Law practice in full swing, I fall blindly into the drug scene. The characters are the same, the names change. Moon, Chris, Lonnie, con-artist, hustlers, swindlers, liars, cheats, all trying to get what benefits them, selfish, self-centered to the extreme, just like me. I'm still trying to find the best dope and the easy lay. I start out snorting coke every weekend. I meet a guy, Chris, who turns me on to crack. I love it! I search the early morning hours in the projects for the next hit of coke or the crack rock that satisfies my mental and physical craving for more. Dope's everywhere; it and the people supplying it find me. I trade dope for legal fees. This is perfectly normal and sane to me. I smoke crack in places I won't normally drive by. I'm always looking in the rearview mirror in fear that the police will pull me over. I am pulled over several times while holding cocaine, pot, and crack, but I'm never searched. I learn how to burn the brillo before inserting the crack rock into the crack pipe. The crack pipe is a glass tube open on both ends and about four inches long. With wear, the glass breaks and eventually ends up about an inch long. Sometimes I don't care whether I burn the brillo or not. And that leaves the taste of copper lingering on my tongue. Craving the next hit I burn my lips on the crack glass before it cools. Then I learn to cool the glass by holding it next to the a/c vent either in the car, apartment or house. I break off antennas from cars and smoke crack out of those. (They're hollow inside) Some of the crack house's I visit have people who offer a dollar for a small rock of crack.

"Hell no," I say.

People stash rocks in their mouth, cigarette packs, socks, and shoes. I buy the glass cylinder with the rose in it at the local mom and pop grocery store. Unbeknown to the non-addicts it is the crack glass in disguise. I run out of dope with no money to buy more. I write bad checks to get more. I search the floor on my hands and knees pulling lint, stones, sheetrock, and carpet hair thinking I might have dropped a piece. This is the life I start to live.

Four months after Susan dies, an attorney friend and I go out drinking. My first ex, Laura, and I are still friendly toward each other and I think it might be a good idea to set my friend, John, up with her. He wants to get laid and I know she's easy. We all end up late at night at Jitterbug's. My friend and ex-wife hit it off from the start. The alcohol and cocaine gives me the courage to approach and flirt with most of the women in the bar. I have enough rejection and decide to leave the lovebirds and go home. I walk by the dance floor when all the lights turn on and women stream towards it.

*A wet t-shirt contest perhaps? Maybe one more beer*, I think.

I stand there and watch the women stream past me. One woman walks by my peripheral vision on the left carrying a red ticket.

"What do you win?" I say to the back of her long blond head. She turns her face towards me and I say, "Hey, I'm John!"

"I'm Teresa." she says smiling and holding her hand out to shake.

"I know, I dreamed about you five years ago!"

"You did not!"

"You don't believe me? Go ask my ex-wife. She's sitting right over there." I say pointing to the table.

We plan our wedding later that night for nine, nine, nineteen ninty-nine. Teresa's five foot four with a china doll complexion, her skin smooth and silky. Her long blonde perm hair floats midway down to her back. Her thick brown eyebrows, perfect porcelain white teeth, and blue eyes are partially covered by bangs that give her a striking natural beauty. Her brilliant face is hidden by thick applications of make-up to cover up the secrets she kept over the years. I constantly correct her thick country accent. Her breasts are naturally supported and her nipples perfectly erect. Her pace is quickened, not realizing she'll never be able to get away from herself. She's a registered nurse currently suspended for stealing drugs from Bibb Medical Center. She's been married twice and has a daughter, Savannah, who is six years old. Her ex-husband has custody. Lortab and cocaine are her drugs of choice. A perfect match!

We go to the Blue Monkey lounge and make out on one of the sofas the rest of the night. I take her home later and we make love long into the night. I'm in love for real this time . . . We're perfect together. She moves into the apartment. I call Mother and tell her I've met my soul mate. I love to stroke her long blonde hair caressing her to sleep at night. Her feet and nails are perfect in shape, rounded and long, big toe symmetrical to the rest, not the short stubby nail less toes of some. The dark hairs on her arms contrast with her porcelain white skin. We love to cuddle on the sofa while watching TV. At night my foot has to be touching hers as we drift off to sleep. We write poems to each other and she slips notes in my pockets before work.

"I love you John. You are the greatest!"

"Thank you! You're a wonderful lover. I love you, Teresa."

We ride to her house in Brent, Alabama, that is next to Centreville where she grew up. On the trip down I'm so blissful the trees sparkle in the light.

I meet her mother who drinks beer with a straw hanging out of a fast food paper cup. She lives with Teresa's grandmother in the house they were all born in. Her brother lives in the single wide mobile home next to the house and reeks of whiskey. Teresa says we'll go in the barn and fuck. We never do. They're all pleased to meet me.

We plan the wedding in the chapel at Canterbury Church. With a one hundred and eighty dollar eight ball of cocaine in my pocket and her supply of Lortab secured, the consummation of the marriage will be phenomenal and long lasting.

"We'll make love all over the Embassy Suites," she says.

"Sweet," say I.

We marry and my parents host the after wedding celebration. I can't wait to leave and snort some coke and fuck all over the hotel. We arrive at the hotel and proceed to consume the freshly bought coke. We snort the entire eight ball in less than an hour. We go to her ex-boyfriend's house to get more. We snort a bunch of cocaine with her ex. I drink lots of beer and anticipate going back to the room. She wants to watch me and her ex have sex. We refuse. She's full of hydrocodone and cocaine and I'm full of myself. We make it back to the room. I'm ready to consummate the marriage.

"My head's killing me! Don't touch me," she says.

"You're shitting me," I say.

I make love to her leg and sleep on the extend-a-bed in the next room.

We move from the apartment to a three-story A-frame house on Dolly Ridge Road. The house is complete with swimming pool, game room, and pool table. It's the perfect house for parties. I reach the American Dream! My law practice is booming, the cocaine, crack, and Lortab are flowing, and we all have good times. No thought of the children. Their innocent eyes see their father stumbling around drunk and stoned. Their noses smell the strange odors radiating from behind the locked bathroom doors. Their ears listen to the snorts of powder cocaine and continuous clicks of lighters igniting the crack rocks from behind the locked bathroom door. No thought of the effects of addiction on others. The drama and chaotic life is the only normal one.

I have numerous close calls with the police. One time coming back from the drug dealer I down several beers, snorted a few lines, and have an eight ball of cocaine in my pocket. I'm pulled over for speeding. The Breathalyzer is broken so the officer makes me get out of the car and walk a straight line. I do the "touch finger to nose with eyes closed" test and pass, so he lets me go. Another time I purchase two ounces of marijuana and run a red light on Highway two-eighty, westbound at the pink package store. The Shelby County sheriff writes me a ticket for speeding as I sit there with the pot in my front left pocket.

It's November of nineteen ninety-nine, Thanksgiving Eve; the children are at their mother's. I just got a new prescription of Klonopin because the cocaine makes me a nervous wreck. Teresa and I drink and snort coke all night as we escape the feelings of restlessness, irritability, and discontent of ourselves. The next morning I come to at the sound of the god-awful ringing of the phone.

"Hello," I muff as the room refuses to stay still.

"Where are you *damn it?*" Mother says sensing the stupor of drugs and alcohol.

Unable to shake Teresa out of her drug-induced coma I proceed to dress haphazardly. I place one sock and two shoes on as my children enter the house. There are beer cans everywhere. An empty tray in the middle of the floor is littered with McDonald straws cut in half. The children get in the car with me and I attempt to drive to Mother's house for Thanksgiving lunch. I'm in a daze and fog. I'm unable to steer and swerve to miss a local mailbox. I pull over and let my oldest son drive the rest of the way. He's fourteen.

I stumble up the stairs at mother's house and an argument ensues as to the state of mind I'm in. I grab a turkey leg and return to the car. Mother, bless her heart, hesitantly allows the children back in the car and we take off down the hill. Still unable to coordinate the steering mechanism I swerve and the children scream, *"Watch out!"* I narrowly miss a neighbor walking her dog. She yells something at me as I yell back while flipping her off. I strike the curb and blow out the front right tire of the runaway train. We ride the rim across the street and stop in an empty parking lot to change the tire. I get out to change the tire forgetting that I previously had shredded the spare from the last debacle. The sirens in the distance are getting louder. The Mountain Brook police pull into the parking lot, guns drawn. They order me to blow in the Breathalyzer. They're puzzled why the device won't register anything as I'm unable to walk or talk coherently. Still puzzled, they pat me down and pull out the bottle of Klonopin, not so hiding in my pocket.

"What's wrong with you?" Mother asks appearing out of thin air.

"He's on cocaine," Johnny quips.

Full of last night's Klonopin they cuff me and I'm charged with DUI. They take me to jail as mother, children, and disabled car watch me leave. I vaguely remember yelling and cussing the police in the cell as they bring me some sort of Thanksgiving dinner that night. I violently throw the food back at them and demand they release me. (Klonopin makes you mean). By midnight my mind clears enough to walk and talk coherently and they release me. I don't remember who picked me up. I go back to the house and notice something missing. Teresa. I call her ex-boyfriend and he materializes the missing pieces of the puzzle. After they took me to jail my mother brought the children back to the house. They awaken the sleeping Klonopin filled beast. A fight ensues and Teresa tries to push Mother over the rail of the deck. Mother hits her over the head with the police summoned telephone. Jail or detox were her choices and she chooses the latter.

I think, *I'll get some rest and pick her up in the morning.*

*What is Mother going to think about me?*

*Why did this happen to me?*

*How could I do this to the children?*

*I hate myself,* I think, as the justification continues and we spend the fourteen hundred dollars rent money on a three-week cocaine binge. (Still can't remember what happened to that turkey leg I ripped off the turkey.)

The children are taken to their mother's and Teresa is forbidden from contact with her daughter. We just recently convinced her ex to let us have custody of Savannah. My parents ban me from contacting them. My childhood best friend calls during this time and tells me he knows what I'm doing late at night. And if I didn't stop, he'd come over and physically remove me from my house. The secret life I hid from everyone is exposed. The sane idea that we move to Teresa's hometown of Centreville seems logical. To get away from all the drugs, dealers, and chaos is the solution. The only problem is that I'm going with us.

Just prior to the move Teresa's sitting in the den and says, "I'm pregnant."

And I say, "It's your decision and I'll support it however you decide."

"Abortion. It's my body and I decide what happens." How selfish, self-centered that is! As Mother would say, "You should have thought about that before you spread your legs." The physical, spiritual, emotional, and psychological trauma that abortion wrecks on a human being is lifelong. I have only witnessed it. The Russians have taken a photograph of the moment a sperm enters an egg. A burst of light happens at that very moment. Is this when the eternal being "jumps" into the biological unit? Aren't we all beings of light, pure consciousness having a third dimensional experience? I think so. Life begins at conception.

We drive to Atlanta and she has the procedure done while I wait in the dimly lit room of the gas chamber, dead babies hanging all around me. We sink deeper into an even greater morass of self-destruction.

A few weeks later, we pack in the middle of the night and move. We settle into a nice double wide on a secluded lot in West Blockton, Alabama where we start over. We celebrate the move at her uncle's house where he provides us with a batch of the best moonshine he's ever made. On the way back to the trailer Teresa gets so mad at me for getting drunk that she tries to sideswipe my side of the car against an embankment. We arrive at the trailer arguing and fighting as I go and get in the bed. She wants to go back to the party and I won't give her the car keys. She jumps on top of me and starts to hit me in the face. Raised in a southern gentleman's home the thought of hitting a woman is taboo. Moonshine overrode those taboos and I uncontrollably throw her off of me and begin to beat her. In a drunken rage I throw her against the wall and she falls on the ground. I kick and cuss her. I then take her head and slam it against the floor over and over. I get up and start walking out the door. She jumps on my back and I throw her on the ground. I get out the door of the mobile home and try to open the car door. She jumps on my back. I fling her off onto the driveway. I start kicking her while she is on the ground and then get in the car and lock the door. As I leave she throws rocks at the windshield. I'm smiling as the harmless pellets strike the windshield. I retreat to the only place I know, a "friend's" house where crack silences the pangs of broken taboos.

I return to the scene of the crime the following day. The guilt of the night before makes me want to drive into the pond across from the mobile home. She lay on the sofa, beaten, bruised, and still in shock.

*Nothing that a crack rock couldn't make better*, I think.

I'm relieved she didn't call the police and angry that her ex-boyfriend came over and tended to her after I left. I pay a visit to the local dealer whom Teresa had found when we moved. As it turns out, West Blockton is the crack capitol of the Southeast! Relief of my tormented mind comes at once with the first hit.

The year of two thousand consists of crack binges, looking for crack, thinking of crack, and swearing off crack. On numerous occasions I would come to the next morning after a binge. I'd throw the crack pipe in the woods. I swear to fucking God, I'll never do that again, I say and mean it. If you hooked me up to a lie detector it would register, "He's telling the truth." We search for crack in the early morning hours. When we didn't buy any from the local crack dealer, he comes over wondering if there's anything wrong. He would give us samples. It's all good he'd say. We go to the crack dealer's house and watch him cook it. We buy it right out of the pan! There are more fights and arguments. I smash furniture, throw objects through the window. I put my fist through the walls and doors. There are reports of missing persons, both her and me. I spend all my gas money on crack and have no way to get to work the next day. We dent and wreck our cars. Those fucking birds chirping mean only one thing; that the sun's coming up. How I hate those damn birds.

There's a neighborhood north of town where the drug dealers hang out and wait on cars to drive by. It's like a crack drive-thru! I'd picked up a twelve hundred fee in the form of a check earlier in the day. I go there one night after we run out of crack. I'm in my bare feet because I know I'm not going to get out of the car. I see a dealer on the road and stop in the middle of the street. He comes over to my window and we negotiate for a ten-dollar rock. I pull my wallet out and take out a bill. We exchange bill and rock at the same time.

He looks at it and says, "That's a dollar bill."

I say, "Shit," as I pull my wallet back out and he grabs it and starts to run.

I jump out of the car and run after him. It's dark and I'm running down the street barefooted and screaming for him to stop. I hear gunshots and duck. The motherfucker is shooting at me. I decide to give up the chase. I go back to the trailer and luckily still have the dope. I pull it out and put in the pipe and light it. It's sheetrock.

We get home one night from the crack dealer. We have a rock about the size of a marble. Teresa likes to hold the crack. We get in the trailer and she says she's dropped the crack and can't find it. I get a flashlight and go out to the car and comb the carpet of the car looking for it. I pull the back seat out of the car even though neither one of us had been in the back seat. It's not in the car so I get on my hands and knees and search the gravel driveway. Two hours pass and I finally give up. I go back in the house and find Teresa in the bedroom smoking it.

One night we shoot up some Dilaudid and decide to get in the garden tub. I come to just as Teresa is slowly submerging under the water. This proves to be a bad idea. I pull her out of the tub and lay her on the bed. We're both fucked up and I spend several hours playing with her naked body. She hardly moves but remembers what I do. On another fiasco I arrive home after work and find her passed out on the floor. She drank a whole bottle of Tussionex cough syrup. I rationalize going to get some dope. We get relief from the madness by continuous hits from the crack pipe or "glass dick" as some call it. Still another time we're drinking and smoking dope and I take some Klonopin to go to sleep. She doesn't want me to go to sleep for some reason and keeps pulling the covers off of me. I pull the covers back over me and she continues to pull them off. This continues for a while and I've finally had enough. I push her off the bed with my foot and she falls and lands on her wrist. It snaps like a twig. She calls her mother to come take her to the ER. I go to sleep.

She moves in with her mother and I move to Birmingham to live with my law partner who has a spare bedroom. My drinking and using don't slow down, but my law practice does. I continue to try and "get her back" but her mother refuses to let me talk to her. Three weeks pass and I finally convince her to talk. She's still in a pink cast when we meet at her mother's house. We decide to go back to the trailer and reconcile. The power is turned off. The fireplace provides the heat and light. We agree to work things out and stay together. We have great make-up sex. A few days (or weeks) later the children are brought back to live with us. Their addicted mother is no longer able to care for them.

The addiction continues its wrath on all of us. We retreat to the bedroom, the bathroom, and sneak outside to hit the crack pipe. I sniff a lot while at the same time flicking the lighter. I think I'm covering the sound of the lighter. We leave the sleeping children alone in the middle of the night to meet dope dealers in Birmingham. Oftentimes I'd give one of the local dope dealers my Seiko watch to hold until I can get them some money. I leave Hoyt in the car while I go inside the dealers' homes to buy dope. I tell him I'm meeting a client for work.

There's no food (or very little) in the house. The electricity is cut off constantly and the phone is disconnected for non-payment. We have no money, spending what little we did have to buy dope. These problems can be resolved by another hit.

We're living like animals. We burn the trash in the lot next to the house. We have more arguments and fist holes in the walls. One day I come home while the children are at school and find blood all over the carpet near the air intake grate. Teresa had ripped it out with her bare hands thinking a crack rock had dropped down in it. I smoke crack with my son. He's fifteen.

Our love's invincible. A birthday poem she writes reads:
"Happy Birthday"
Happy birthday to you sweetheart
Here's hoping this year will be the greatest,
For I will be there right beside you
Through the good, the happy or even what we have shared the latest.
I knew that when our eyes first met that *you* were my real soul mate,
Together through life hand in hand
Somehow we would make it with faith.
You say you dreamed of me years and years ago
That one day we would be together,
Thank God that time has passed
And now it shall be forever.

Years will come as birthdays do
That's just part of life,
But I'll stand proud and secure
Just knowing I am your wife.
I love you,
Teresa-June fourteenth, two thousand.

# Chapter Six

## *An Act of Providence*

I leave the dope dealer's apartment in Southside at about seven o'clock one night. The crack pipe and dope are securely hidden in the front left pocket. I pull out of the complex in front of a slow moving car. I can't wait to get back to the trailer to smoke it. The blue lights ignite from the slow moving car and cause nerves to shock and electrify my crack-ridden body. My mind scrambles for excuses. I pull over and reach for my driver's license like I'd done many times before. I make a quick check on the dope in my pocket making sure it's secure.

"Step out of the car," he orders.

"I'm a lawyer," I plead with the hope that he'd just let me go.

"Please step out of the car."

*Fuck*, I think, as my hand fidgets around the illegal pocket.

"What's in your pocket, a weapon?" he says as he pat's me down revealing the hidden treasure.

They call the Narcotics unit, cuff me and place me in the back of the squad car while they ransack my vehicle. *The Birmingham News* police blotter, September twentieth, two thousand reads, "Seventeenth Street South, thirteen hundred block, September twelfth, eight thirty-five p.m., forty-three year old West Blockton man arrested in connection with possession of controlled substance." Mother later confides to me she knew "the forty-three year old man" was her son. They'd been planning my funeral at Elmwood cemetery.

I'm placed on TASC (Treatment Alternative to Street Crime) and random drug testing through the court. I call every day for my color code and if my color comes up, I have to report for a urine screen. I'm such a brilliant lawyer I think I can beat the system. I continue my case indefinitely. People tell me to drink lots of water, pickle juice, beer, and Clorox. I know that it takes seventy-two hours to get the cocaine out of my system. I use and then pray that my color won't come up. I get away with it for a while and test clean. I get my case continued several more times. I drink capfuls of Clorox mixed with water. I find out later that

I'm supposed to put the Clorox in the urine sample, not drink it.

I walk into court the day my case is set. I pull my file from the bailiffs' cabinet and sit at the counselor's table and wait for the judge to call the case.

I'm thinking, *What's the Judge going to think of me?*

*How did I get here?*

*What will happen to me?*

*Will I be able to practice law?*

*There's no way out now.*

*I'm fucked.*

"John, what have you got today?" The drug court judge quips from his throne.

"Can we go into your office?" I say avoiding eye contact as I follow him, head down, into his chamber.

I close the door and sit down across from him and slowly hand him my file. He opens it and turns white as a ghost, his eyes widen as he leans forward and says, "This is you."

"I know," I say still avoiding eye contact.

"You know I'm going to have to report this to the bar."

"I know."

"You need to call Squire," he says.

I call Squire that day and set up an appointment to go see him, whoever he is.

A few days later I go to his office and he tells me how he'd been a terrible drunk and had to give up his law license a decade ago. He worked for seven years as a clerk in a hotel while he got sober. He thinks I need to work in a hotel so I can get some humility. I sit across from him telling him all about my "problems" and start to cry.

"John, you just need to grow up!" he says in a gruff, angry voice.

Some weeks later the unsatisfied cravings continue unabated. Teresa walks in the door after coming back from the dope dealer's house. Dirty and bruised but otherwise unharmed I ask for the dope.

She says, "I ran off the road. The dope is somewhere in the car and we need to find it before the police get there."

We scurry down the steep embankment where the totaled car lay. We frantically search through the debris and ground leaving empty handed.

The late night binges continue. The Alabama State Bar puts me in outpatient treatment where they give me Antabuse (Antabuse causes you to become violently sick if you drink alcohol) to prevent me from drinking. I attend a class where I meet other alcoholics and addicts. We all share stories and ways we think we can beat the system. Some confide to me how they take the Antabuse and then go sit by the emergency room and drink. I'm introduced to my bar monitor and eventual

AA sponsor who reports to the bar on my mental status.

"This one is not going to make it," he writes. He confides to me that he'd come to every morning and grab his half-gallon bourbon bottle to calm the shakes. One morning he drops the bottle and it shatters on the floor. As he's licking the bourbon off the floor the liquid begins to turn red. Bewildered, he soon realizes that his tongue is being cut as he laps up the glass laden precious juice. He surmises that placing a straw in the bottle and putting it in the refrigerator will solve the problem!

I think, *What a sick bastard*! (As I'm living like an animal).

He takes me to my first AA meeting in Hoover. I vaguely remember the welcoming atmosphere of that first meeting. He buys me a Big Book. The people he introduces to me at the meeting write their names and phone numbers. I drive back to the mobile home and thumb through the book.

I think, *Who wants to read about a bunch of drunks*?

It makes a great beer coaster. I recall the multiple circles the cans of Budweiser left on the cover. Teresa gives that book to her mother who later dies from complications of alcohol poisoning.

The following week I'm drinking, driving, and smoking crack. Teresa and I park in a wooded area at the end of a dirt road near the double wide.

I run out of my portion (we had started to halve the amount when we'd buy the dope) and I ask her for a push. (The push is when you push the brillo through the crack pipe to the other end of the pipe causing the brillo to catch the resin from the dope.). I start to argue and plead my case about all the times I had given her *my* push. She becomes adamant that she's not going to give me any. She tells me that I smoked my portion up and should smoke it slower. I start the car and slam it into reverse and turn around. I fly down the dirt road and punch the accelerator to the floor.

I think, *I'm going to sideswipe her side of the car.*

The next thing I remember is coming to and the car's upside down. She's lying unconscious next to me, crumpled up on the ceiling of the car. The ceiling has about two to three inches of dirt where the car acted like an earth scraper. I wake her up and extricate us from the vehicle. She won't talk to me.

I keep saying, "I didn't mean to."

"It was an accident."

"I was just trying to scare you."

"Are you OK?"

She's walking kind of funny and the silent treatment continues. We walk to the trailer and open the door. The children are standing there. They heard the noise of the crash. I have a four-inch gash on the top of my head and it's bleeding down my face. We have dirt all over us. She has a broken hip and cracked vertebrae in her neck that emanate no pain, the cocaine providing the analgesic. We go to the bedroom and lock the door to finish off what we had started. She proceeds to hit the crack pipe. She tells me I tried to kill her. I remind her of the time she tried to kill me. She goes in the bathroom and pulls some dope out of her jeans. I accuse her of holding out on me and I need a hit. I go and get some beer out of the refrigerator and return to the boxing ring. We continue to yell while the children stand outside the door and listen. I'm sitting on the bed chugging beers in between yells. She grabs one of the beers and pours it over my head. I stand up and slam my fist through the antique dresser my Uncle Sam had given me. I push her out of the bedroom into the presence of my children and barricade myself in the bedroom by placing the smashed dresser in front of the door. She then proceeds to beat on the door and threatens to call the police if I don't let her in. I decide it's probably a good time to leave. I just totaled our last car. We had her uncle's "three on a tree" pickup truck he had let us borrow for me to get to work. I grab what is left of the six-pack out of the refrigerator and speed from the scene. She calls the police and I almost make it to the interstate when they pull me over. I get arrested. Again.

I spend several hours in the drunk tank at the Bibb County jail. I convince the jailer that I need to go to the hospital because I injured my head in the accident and have a terrible headache. They transport me to Bibb County Medical Center where I plan my escape. I'm treated, released, and walk home. I hitchhike back to the trailer and find Teresa unable to move. She's called Laura who had come to her aide, I'm sure, with pain pills. The children are there.

"Look at what you have done to her."

"Why did you do this to her?"

"She can't move."

"She needs to go to the hospital and you just left her here." They all say pugnaciously.

They take her to Druid City Hospital in Tuscaloosa. I'm alone and I turn to the only solution I know . . . more dope. I'm forbidden to contact Teresa at the hospital because she has put a restraining order against me. I proceed to get high and drunk. I hear a knock on the door. The officer stands there holding a warrant.

"You're under arrest," he says.

"You're shitting me," I say just freshly released from confinement that morning.

He takes me to jail this time without the cuffs as they're getting to know me. She'd filed reckless endangerment charges.

I persuade the jailers once again to release me, this time on my own recognizance and I walk back to the empty trailer.

*I didn't mean to wreck the car.*

*It was an accident.*

*I didn't mean to hurt her.*

*Does she still love me?*

*Will she love me again?* I think as the feelings of dejection and rejection are forgotten into the oblivion of the next drink and drug.

In fear of losing my license to practice law, already in jeopardy, I contact my sponsor a few days later.

"What happened to you last Thursday night? You were supposed to go to a meeting with me," he says with an air of concern and experience.

"I had a little car trouble," I tell him while remembering the car that lay in a junkyard up the street.

I take the children to see the car. They look up at me with tears streaming down their angry faces while the twisted mangled heap of metal stands as a silent sentinel of a miracle. It looks like it had been put in a trash compactor. Several weeks later Teresa is discharged from the hospital and calls to come pick her up. Ecstatic, I arrive at her room to see her in a neck brace and barely able to walk. She has to walk with the help of the polio type crutches. I'm devastated at the sight of her

battered body. We drive home in the pickup. I
have a scratched face and four stitches in my head.

# Chapter Seven

## *The Compound*

*"Our deepest fear is not that we are inadequate. Our deepest fear is that we are powerful beyond measure. It is our light, not our darkness, that most frightens us. We ask ourselves, who am I to be brilliant, gorgeous, talented and fabulous? Actually, who are you not to be? You are a child of God. Your playing small doesn't serve the world. We were born to make manifest the glory of God that is within us. It's not just in some of us; it's in everyone. And as we let our own light shine, we unconsciously give other people permission to do the same. As we are liberated from our own fear, our presence automatically liberates others."*
-Marianne Williamson

"Go to Rehab or give up your law license," the State Bar commands.

"Where?" I ask.

"Cornerstone of Recovery," they respond.

I'm pissed off because I have to quit using and drinking but at the same time I'm relieved knowing that I don't have to live like this anymore. I take Johnny to the Psychiatric Ward at UAB. They lock him in a room to prevent him from hurting him or me. He screams and cusses me as I leave. I go buy some dope. I get home and wait on the treatment van coming the next day. Teresa's in her neck brace and she hobbles over to the bed. I sit on the bed with her. Hoyt's asleep in his room. We proceed to smoke the small crack rock I purchased on the way home. The only effect I get is numb lips. I can't even get high anymore. It's November fifteenth, two thousand.

The next morning I have a court case in Bessemer where a client pays me three hundred dollars. I go back to the trailer with the money and give it to Teresa. The van arrives and I leave West Blockton sleepless and expecting room service at the treatment center. We arrive at the compound in Maryville, Tennessee. The driver is "jonesin" from all the crack stories I relay to him during the five-hour drive. I'm wired, broken, and weigh one hundred and sixty pounds. I'm still not quite ready to surrender.

*It wasn't that bad.*

*I don't have to practice law anymore. I can teach.*

*I can't believe this is happening to me.*

*I need to call my parents; maybe they will love me now,* I think as I minimize, deny, and rebel.

Leaving Teresa nearly crippled and with the vision of Hoyt dressed in summer clothes waiting for the bus in freezing weather tear more holes in my heart. He's twelve.

They put me in de-tox. They take my picture. They take my blood pressure. They take my blood. They take my urine. I'm weighed, splayed and neutered. I complete questionnaires that ask the same questions over and over again.

"Were you abused as a child?"

"What are the earliest memories you have of sexual activity?"

"Do you have any memories of being touched by an adult?"

We have "groups" where the counselors confront us about our rationalizations and justifications for drinking and using. Rationalization and justification is like masturbation, you're only fucking yourself.

"You're the Queen of De Nile."

"You're minimizing your drug use."

"Quit acting like Queen Baby."

We have daily AA meetings and trips to Wal-Mart to buy cigarettes and supplies. We flirt.

People get thrown out for having sex in the laundry room. Others sneak across the railroad tracks to have sex in the woods. They're trying to substitute the euphoria of drugs for the euphoria of sex. I'm thrust into the world of recovery with seven cents in my pocket. I'm mentally withdrawing from cocaine. I'm unable to sleep. I repeat the Serenity Prayer and the Lord's Prayer in bed every night until I drift off to dream of smoking crack. "I'm screwed, blued, and tattooed," as Mother would say.

We all talk about our "dramas" and our "situations." One woman talks about how she takes one hundred and twenty Lortab a day. Another speaks of spending thousands of dollars a day on her crack habit. Still another throws a boulder on her foot so she can get a script for pain meds. Some people come in and stay three days or a week just to detox off the drugs and alcohol. They're unable to put a complete sentence together. I fight being there. I swear to leave. I pack and I unpack my shambled suitcase numerous times. I plan to leave with two women who offer me a ride. In my thoughts I replay, justify, and rationalize every scenario possible. I whine about my job, my family, and my future. People talk about the committee in their head; I talk about the United Nations in mine. I exhaust myself.

We have fun at the ropes course that consists of walking a rope above the ground and having teams help each other across it. We sometimes laugh so hard at the insanity of it all. We get serious and we get silly. We take a day trip to a go-cart course in Gatlinburg.

Family day arrives and I think, *Why won't they come see me?*

*Do they still hate me?*

I'm unable to communicate with my wife because the phone is disconnected. I advise the counselors to come and get me when Teresa calls so I can talk to her. I get notes from her that say, "I Love You." The counselors decide I need to wear a sign every day that says, "Ask me how I'm feeling." I have no clue what feelings are.

"How are you feeling today, John?" fellow inmates ask.

"I don't know; let me look at my list," I say while reaching in my back pocket to pull out a list of feeling descriptions.

I serve three weeks of my thirty-five day confinement when Teresa and my children move in with her sister, husband, and their two children in a singlewide mobile home located in a car junkyard just outside of Centreville on Highway eighty-two.

The counselors tell me, "John, you've been drinking and using for thirty years and we think you need to stay up here in a halfway house for four months."

"I can't," I say. "I need to get back and save my family."

I think, *I'll show them. I'll just leave here and go get fucked up!*

I'm three weeks sober (longer than I've ever been) and somewhat clearer minded. I reflect back for a moment on all the destruction I wrought and cry out in my mind to God, *Please remove this craving from me!* And I mean it for the first time ever. He lifts it right out of me! I don't realize this at the time, but looking back, God is doing for me what I did not have the power to do myself. I didn't know I could use God!

We have a therapy session where we all drew an example of our addiction. I start on the left side of the paper and draw a building in shambles with smoke and flames coming out of the top. The next image I draw is a car turned upside down and on fire. Moving from left to right I draw an image of the rehab building. The final image is superman flying away.

"That's very good, John," the counselor says.

I start a guided meditation group. It's mostly women of course. I lay them down on the floor and in my monotone voice I relax them. I learned this meditation when I was with Susan:

"Relax the muscles in the top of your head with each exhale. Now relax the muscles in your neck and shoulders, down into the chest and stomach, down into your legs and feet, relax thoroughly, comfortably relaxed . . . now imagine a red ball of light at the base of your spine. Bring your breath to this area and imagine it getting bigger like a balloon with each breath you take. As you breathe out, imagine all your pain, worries, and fears leaving your body as dark specks of light. Repeat this for five breaths. Now move up to your navel area and imagine an orange ball of light. Repeat the breath exercise. Now, move up to your solar plexus and imagine a golden yellow ball of light and repeat the breath exercise. Continue upward to the heart and imagine an emerald green ball of light breathing in the love of God and out any negative thoughts or feelings. Now, move up to the throat area and imagine a blue ball of light and repeat the breath exercise. The next area is between the eyes and its color is black light purple repeating the breath exercise. Now, move up to the top of the head and imagine a violet ball of light and repeat the breath exercise. Now, breathe deep and on the exhale, imagine the darkness as specks coming out of you while chanting "Ohm."

"That's better than sex," they say.

I coined out (a term they use in rehab where you get a coin the day before you are released) after thirty-five days and the counselors tell me to get a sponsor, go to ninety meetings in ninety days and work steps. I call my monitor and tell him I need a sponsor. I tell him I need someone who's done drugs and can relate to me, not an alcoholic.

I'm thinking, *Will I make it without using again?*

*This place is safe.*

*Can I use recreationally?*

*I can shoot some heroin one time, just to see what it is like.*

*What will Teresa do, will she get sober?*

"I'll be your temporary sponsor until you can find someone like that" he says.

"Okay," I say. "That sounds reasonable."

Everyone signs my twelve thousand dollar AA Big Book:

"John, God blessed me by putting you in my life when he did. I have grown a lot from listening to you. I am a little afraid for you going out there & I hope you have *fear* also-you need to & don't ever lose it. So what you know it's going to take to not go down that dead-end road again. I know you can do it! Your loving friend, Cathy from Kentucky."

"Dear John, remember you are a good person. Bad things do not make bad people. *Love yourself! Love God*! Serenity, Courage and Wisdom. I love you man." Issac. Ashville.

"John, you have touched me in so many ways! I love you, God loves you. Thank you for your friendship. Keep it simple, stupid." Pamela.

"John, you are such a loving and caring man! You are blessed to have a wonderful wife to share your life with. I want you to know how much I appreciate you listening to me and helping me as an attorney and friend. You make me feel good just being there & of course your *meditations*! Remember what brought you here and know you don't want to go back down that same road! Best wishes to you and your family & you will always be remembered in my prayers." Love you! Stephanie.

"What we are does not count-What we do today does! The skirt waits. Rick. (Referring to the skirt you had to wear if you relapsed. Rick was a counselor who would dress up as a woman and suck cock for rock before he got sober, thus "the skirt").

My temporary sponsor makes me write on the inside cover of my AA book, "I am not unique. I am not the only fuck-up in AA!"

I arrive in Birmingham by bus late in the night after a fourteen-hour trip. Teresa and her sister are there to greet me. She's cut the long blonde hair I used to lovingly brush and caress! I'm homeless, car-less, and clueless as we arrive at her sister's trailer at the aforementioned junkyard. Eight of us are crammed into a two-bedroom singlewide. We make bed pallets in the den for the children to sleep on. Teresa and I stay in the back bedroom. Teresa is taking Klonipin to sleep and

God knows what else. I play with her body and masturbate after she falls asleep, knowing she's too fucked up to feel me.

My sponsor suggests I read pages eighty-six through eighty-eight in the AA book every morning and say the third-step prayer on my knees. Instead, I read pages eighty-three through eighty-eight (this Intelligence is already guiding me) and read the third-step prayer, not on my knees, still not quite ready to completely surrender. I tell Teresa it's *her* turn to go to rehab and get sober, but she wants no part of it, although she does go to an occasional meeting with me in Hoover. I start an AA meeting at a church in Woodstock where one woman shows up for the first and only meeting.

I work part time at my sponsor's office. Teresa's cousin let us use his Toyota Celica. The motor ran well, but the brakes eventually go out. I'm driving to Birmingham for work and meetings with no brakes! The car has a five speed and I can gear down to slow up and pull on the emergency brake to stop completely if I have to. God is surely watching out for me. My sponsor takes meetings to Montclair Hospital and I go with him. I tell my story of what it was like, what happened, and what it's like now. I start to work the twelve steps. I start to get peace.

I meet with Jean Marie who is the head of the Lawyers Helping Lawyers program at the State bar. I'm incapable of practicing law, so I put myself on disability inactive status. This requires me to attend meetings and go to the lawyers monitoring group. These consist of other recovering lawyers. The therapist keeps the bar advised of my progress. Being placed on inactive status gives me some humility. My sponsor, Trevor, who's also my bar monitor writes status reports to the bar.

My sponsor instructs me to read the Doctors Opinion and Chapter One. Memorize the steps verbatim. Compare and contrast the spiritual ideals on page twenty-seven and the spiritual experience in the back of the book.

Shit, I can hardly put a complete sentence together!

If I miss one word in my memorization of the steps he says, "God damn it, I told you verbatim."

Other people in the program call him an AA Nazi. It's just what I need.

It's around January twentieth, two thousand, I'm working steps and going to meetings. I come home one night after an AA meeting and Teresa and I get into an argument.

"*Get out!*" She says, realizing that I'm getting sober and she wants no part of it.

"I can't believe it! After all I've done for you. How can you do this to me?" I yell.

Johnny had been released from the psych ward while I was still in treatment. The children are terribly sick and have a fever of 105. The next morning I amble over to the Amoco station across the street and call my parents to come and get us. It takes me all morning to reach them. I throw all our stuff into plastic garbage bags. The small rack of clothes we have left and my twenty-five inch Sanyo TV are put on the steps as we wait on our ride out of the junkyard. I recall sitting at the Amoco station in complete defeat. I surrender.

I realize at that moment where my self-will has gotten me and say while looking up in the sky, "Ok God, you can take it from here!"

I worked the first three steps of Alcoholics Anonymous:

"We admitted we were powerless over alcohol, that our lives had become unmanageable."

"Came to believe that a power greater than myself could restore us to sanity."

"Made a decision to turn our will and our life over to the care of God as we understood him." Or the short version, I can't, He can, I think I'll let Him.

I'm forty-three year's old living with my parents, no job, no car, and know nothing. I catch rides to meetings and work steps with my sponsor. I meet with the deacon at The Church at Brook Hills where Susan and I attended (they remembered her) and convince them to give me three hundred dollars. I find a car in Centreville for three hundred dollars and talk the guy down to two hundred and fifty. It's a nineteen eighty-six Ford Thunderbird with no front grill, no muffler, bald tires, and manual defrost. I'm coming back from Centreville when the front right tire blows out.

*That fucking bitch.*

*This is all Teresa's fault,* I think while I walk the two miles to the Bessemer exit and call Dad to come pick me up.

By God that car gets me to meetings! I drive up to the meeting place, the car's smoking; the people are smoking. I think they're laughing at me! They aren't laughing at me because they're too busy thinking about themselves!

I ask for jobs at the meetings and I hear that Serra Oldsmobile in Centerpoint is hiring car salesman. Actually car dealerships are always hiring car salesman! I interview for the job and they hire me. I am a used car salesman/attorney, so nobody believes a word I say. The hustling, lying, cheating, and greed of the car business is appalling. Most of the salesmen are pumped up on pills and cocaine. Fortunately for me I work where the home office is located and there's less of that there. I'm working six days a week, twelve hours a day, and the boys and I move to Pinson. I'm receiving government-assisted housing. The fan strategically placed by my bed drowns the gunshots, fights, and drug deals going on in the courtyard below my window. It's not where you are, it's who you are where you are!

The children ages sixteen and twelve, are left alone to fend for themselves after school while I work the program, sell cars during the day, and go to meetings at night. The Centerpoint group meeting on Tuesday nights take bets on whether I'll stay sober or not. (Common judgment calls in AA!). Phone calls to my sponsor, working steps, and reading the Big Book keep my sanity.

One afternoon while sitting in the apartment watching my twenty-five inch Sanyo, Hoyt comes screaming down the stairs, "Johnny cut himself and is laying in the tub bleeding to death!"

I run upstairs and open the bathroom door to see Johnny lying in blood red colored water, cut marks on his wrist and semi-conscious. He leaps out of the water and starts to fight me. I tell Hoyt to dial nine one one. Johnny is crying out for help.

Receipt of stolen property is what they charge Hoyt with. "I didn't know it was stolen Daddy," he tells me. Apparently, one of the local "gangs" were breaking into houses and storing it at our apartment. The children learned from their father how to manipulate, justify, and lie. Who can blame them after all?

My eyes open in the morning and my first thought is, *I hate her.*

*She threw me out of the junkyard.*

*I haven't heard from her.*

*Who is she living with?*
*Who is she fucking?*
*What is she doing?*
*God damn her*! And then I start to pray for her peace, happiness, and prosperity. Every night whether I hate her or love her, I pray for her anyway. The hatred begins to dissipate. I work step four, "Made a searching and fearless moral inventory of ourselves."
I make four columns listing each person on a separate page whom I'm angry at.
First Column;
I am angry with:
John.
Second Column;
Why am I angry?
I put myself in a position to be hurt. My perfectionism caused me to have unrealistic expectations. I wanted to have sex all the time. I was a caretaker and co-dependent. I lost my attorney status.
Third Column;
What does this affect?
My self-esteem and pride; sex relations; security; ambition; pocket book.
Fourth Column;
The fourth column is my part in the anger:
I was selfish, self-centered, and self-seeking and only wanted to please myself. I wanted a perfect wife who was beautiful. I wanted a perfect life

with perfect children. I have let my sex drive completely control my life. I wanted someone to take care of so she would love me and treat me good. I was active in my addiction and didn't care about anybody else.

The next page is Teresa.

She threw me out of the junkyard!

**What was affected?**

Self-esteem. Pride; sex relations; emotional security.

**My Part:**

I demanded sex all the time. I broke her arm, broke her neck, broke her shoulder and broke her hip.

*Shit*! No wonder she threw me out of the trailer! My sponsor almost fell out of his chair laughing so hard! Hell, I married her! Who's at fault? Putting everything down on paper I saw that all the people I was angry with had a common denominator, me! I didn't want to look at myself, as I perceived everyone else was at fault. Going down the list of people whom I had resentment against I saw where I had been at fault.

Step five, "Admitted to God, to ourselves, and to another human being the exact nature of our wrongs."

Having told my sponsor everything "they" had done to me, he leaned back in his chair and asked, "What is the worst thing you have ever done in your life that you swore you would never tell anyone and that you would take to your grave?"

Shit, I didn't know I needed to tell him *all* my secrets! I tell him (but I can't tell you because they will send me to prison) and the relief is instant. I'm free from all my secrets.

Completing step five, I left my sponsor's office. The fifth step promises come true.

"We pocket our pride and go to it, illuminating every twist of character, every dark cranny of the past. Once we have taken this step, withholding nothing, we are delighted. We can look the world in the eye. We can be alone at perfect peace and ease. Our fears fall from us. We begin to feel the nearness of our Creator. We may have had certain spiritual beliefs, but now we begin to have a spiritual experience . . ." *Alcoholics Anonymous.*

I walk down Second Avenue a free man. I had confided all of my secrets to another human being and saw where I'd been at fault. I'd never been this high without dope; it frightens me. That night I get drunk and smoke crack! I was afraid of the light. I was used to the dark. It's March twenty-fourth, two thousand and one.

# Chapter Eight

## *Endings and Beginnings*

I continue to sell cars and actually get pretty good at it. I pull a "hat trick" (that's selling three cars in one day) at the "confiscated car" sale. The cars aren't actually confiscated. They're pulled from other car lots and the dealership tells the customers that the police had confiscated them! What lies people believe!

"Maybe I'll find some money in the trunk!" the customers say.

I know the cars because when they're brought in to the dealership, the mechanics tell me what's wrong with them.

"You don't want that car. The transmission is about to go out." I tell prospective customers. They appreciate that.

On September eleventh, two thousand one, I arrive at the dealership. Marianne Serra is watching TV in her office at the back of the showroom. We are notified that a plane has flown into the Twin Towers and everyone's in a state of shock. I receive a phone call from Hoyt's school saying he's absent. I dropped him off at school earlier that morning. Between the events of that day and the anger I still had, I fly to the apartment to find him and a friend watching TV. I take my belt off and give him two or four heavy licks. The terror on his face is forever imprinted on my mind. It's only the second time I whipped him. The first time is when I lived with Shannon in Montgomery. I'm in our apartment and the boys are with me. The Fire Marshall comes to the door and says there'd been a fire at the complex. The kitchen matches left a trail from the fire to our apartment door! I question Hoyt like a prosecutor does a murderer and he finally admits setting the fire. I whip him with a belt. He's five and to this day he denies that he did it.

I have enough of the car business and apply for reinstatement with the bar in the summer of two thousand one. With the Lawyers Helping Lawyers Program and testimony from my sponsor, the panel of decision makers reinstates my license to practice law. I have to wait on the Order from the Supreme Court. Also, around this time, a customer brings in a late model Saturn for trade. It's in great shape and I really need a non-smoking car. I purchase the car for fifteen hundred dollars and the dealership lets me pay fifty a month by payroll deduction.

It's exactly one year to the day of being thrown out the junkyard that I receive the Order from the Supreme Court reinstating me to the practice of law. At about the same time I receive a referral fee of fifteen hundred dollars that gives me enough to rent an office space and re-start my practice. God does not work in mysterious ways. He knows exactly what He's doing.

I'd worked all of the twelve steps, continued to go to meetings, and I was looking for someone to sponsor. I'm full of peace, joy, and happiness. I had found what I've been searching for all my life through sex and money, both of which had left me irritable, angry, frustrated, restless, and discontent. I'm still keeping one secret. I've never told my sponsor or anyone in the meetings about my relapse. This is killing me emotionally. I finally get to that place of pitiful, incomprehensible demoralization. I'm still worried about what other people think of me. I'd picked up my one-year chip in November and by March I can't sleep or eat. I admit to him that I had relapsed.

"You're sober now, aren't you?" he says matter-of-factly.

I change my sobriety date to March twenty-fourth, two thousand one.

My law practice improves and I'm still full of myself. I'm ready to move from the government assisted living conditions.

I think, *I deserve to live in the "better" parts of town, Mountain Brook, Vestavia or Hoover.*

The applications and interviews for houses in those areas are turned down for negative credit. A man in the program has a house for rent in Fultondale.

*I don't want to live in Fultondale with a bunch of rednecks*, I think.

Sitting on three acres of land, the little white house secluded by trees is what God leads me to. It has plenty of room for a vegetable garden and the setting is idyllic. Peaceful, serene, and twelve minutes to the office, yet living in the "country" is better than anything I can imagine. Waking up and going out on the front porch to read my Big Book and other spiritual literature, I *love* to hear the birds chirping as the sun comes up! When I quit trying to run the show, the show starts running.

I graduate from drug court and the felony possession of crack cocaine is dismissed. I go to Centreville to face the charges of reckless endangerment and DUI. I walk in the courtroom and notice the judge. I've seen him in meetings! We all go into his office. I tell them of my recovery and the prosecutor offers to dismiss the reckless endangerment charge and plead to a first time DUI. (It's actually my sixth). I take the offer.

I just settled in to my new home when the Shelby County coroner calls. They brought Teresa in to Shelby County Memorial Hospital DOA. She overdosed on hydrocodone and methadone. I'd not heard from Teresa since she had thrown me out of the junkyard. It had been a year and a half. We never divorced so I'm the next of kin. Her sister wants me to come to the wake. My sponsor doesn't think that is a good idea. I ignored his advice, as usual, and the children and I drive to Centreville.

I arrive at the funeral home and am greeted by her family. They tell me the sordid details of what had happened to her. Her sister tells me that after I left, the rage of addiction had taken control of her. She stayed at the dope house across the street from them. She'd been arrested numerous times and moved in with a dope dealer somewhere in Shelby County. She had lost most of her teeth. She stopped breathing after taking the deadly mixture. The man she's living with offers to pay for the funeral. When I meet him, we both start crying and tell each other how we both loved her. I clear everyone out of the funeral home so I can be alone with her. Lying in the casket, her beautiful china doll face hardly resembles the woman I had dreamed of. I make my amends to her and confess how selfish I'd been. I apologize for hurting her so many times, mentally and physically. The final pangs of guilt and remorse are lifted right out of me. I don't hate her anymore. The gratitude I feel is overwhelming. I realize at that moment that if I had stayed with her, I never would have stayed sober. She saved my life!

# Chapter Nine

## *Don't Play With Magic*

I've always been interested in magic: The ability to control outcomes of people, places, and things. Not the dime store tricks of childhood, but real witchcraft. I had known Eric for several years. He'd seen me in addiction and now sober so he wants me to hypnotize him to raise his psychic abilities. People mistake us for brothers, not because we look anything alike, but our energy vibrations are the same. He's five foot six with long peppered gray hair combed back and big bushy eyebrows. He doesn't know how to wear deodorant. Adorning his fingers are pentagram rings and long fingernails. He makes no bones about his power and I'm afraid of it. He gives me books on hypnosis that I read with enthusiasm or maybe because I'm afraid that he'll hurt me somehow if I don't comply. He told me how he has killed people who crossed him. He's killed animals in the past with his magic, so he says.

I go to visit him one night. He confides to me that he had gotten mad at me a couple of years ago and went to bed angry holding his magic wand. His wand is made of a copper tube nine inches long filled with crystals and magnets. The copper tube is wrapped with leather. He tells me that if he goes to bed angry with somebody while holding his wand bad things will happen to the person he's angry with. He diagrams how his wand is made. He tells me that he did this to me and that is when I wrecked the car.

"You asshole."

"You fucking bastard."

"Why'd you do this?" I question him believing his power.

"I thought it would bring you to your senses," he says.

I'm so intrigued by the power of the wand that I go and make me one the following week.

On another visit he wants to give me some quartz crystals. He brings out a large crystal cluster he had been given years ago. He then breaks several of the crystals off of the large grouping. I'm watching him do this, when one of the pieces lunges several feet over the carpet at his finger and cuts it.

"Damn, what the fuck happened?"

And he says, "I forgot to ask their permission to break it off the cluster. The crystal got mad and cut me."

I have no idea that the crystals are actually alive and would not have believed it if I had not seen the crystal move across the carpet with my own eyes. At ten yards he makes a candle flame move back and forth by moving his hand side to side, the flames dancing in rhythm to his waving hand.

Another friend wants to start a magic meeting group. Fred is Laura's brother-in-law. I am to record the minutes. We meet in my office February, March and April of two thousand six and discuss magic spells. I've always admired him for his abilities. We had done some automatic handwriting when I was married to Laura. Her sister had communicated with their father through "automatic handwriting" (allowing spirit to guide your hand, like a Ouija board) after he had died. I'm told I'll be the leader of The Church According to the Gospel of God and the Light. The meeting minutes are recorded and none of us really have a clue as to what we're doing. I keep a record of the meetings.

February tenth, two thousand six:

We first thanked the spirits for all the gifts we have been receiving.

Magic Club First Meeting Minutes

## First Spell

Named:   Reflecting shield with feelers.

First expand your aura two to four feet around your body. (The aura is the energy field surrounding your body that Kirlian photography can pick up).

Then imagine surrounding your aura with a shield made of titanium and diamonds. Imagine tentacles attached to this shield and expanding from the surface in every direction away from your body, all the same length. Then imagine tiny tentacles attached to the inside of the shield and touching your body. These will pick up energy vibrations that the longer outside tentacles are touching from outside of the shield. Now imagine a second shell around the end of the longer tentacles. The tentacles will pick up negative vibrations and alert you to any negativity that comes your way and the direction it is coming from. The double shielding will protect you from any negativity directed at you.

## End of First Meeting

Second meeting we will try and recognize where energy patterns or vibrations are coming from and try and discern from whom they are coming.

## Second Meeting

March tenth, two thousand six:

We first thanked all the spirits for the gifts we have been receiving.

We discussed the "vapire's." This was a term that Fred made up and is described as dark vapors he has observed coming out of the ground when things started to go wrong. (Murphy's Law, anything that can go wrong will go wrong).

When Murphy's Law begins to happen dark shadows or vapire's begin to come out of the ground. The more things go wrong, the more vapire's will materialize. You can slow these down or eliminate them all together by imagining you are laying down a blanket of fire over the earth. The best defense against these vapire's is having a positive attitude. In contrast when things go good, white "snowflake like" (positron) vapors emanate from the sky and fall to earth.

End of Second meeting.

Third Meeting

April seventh, two thousand six:

We need to *always thank* the spirits that are guiding and directing us.

We had our third member Grace join the group. We discussed what we're doing with her. Grace suggests that we come up with a purpose and a mission statement and I think that's a good idea. We suggest that Grace write one for us. Grace is introduced to "Clyde, Jr." Fred made Clyde several weeks ago during a lightning storm by invoking a spirit into a wooden effigy he'd found in his yard. Clyde is a piece of wood approximately six inches tall and has a natural shaped human head with a body that tapered to a point. We think it is to be used to break chains that are binding us and to bring us stuff. Like money. I used Clyde before and it seemed to work. Grace says she thinks that "Clyde Jr." is not the name of the object and that the name will be revealed to her. She thinks it's a good idea to put Clyde in boiling water to reveal his true identity. Fred is making another object, but does not know yet what it is for.

Before Grace decides to join us she's a little hesitant, but as she's sitting in the chair all she can see outside the window is "Magic." (She's seeing the Lichter's Magic Credit sign on Fourth Ave.) As we're discussing her joining us, a bird hovers outside of the window. According to Grace, this is a "sign" that she's on the correct path and she decides to join the group. We attempt to bring our thoughts in sync at the end of the meeting. We think Grace will greatly contribute to the group and we are excited about her enthusiasm.

End of Third meeting

Fred warns me to bring Clyde back to him within seven days of me using him or bad things will happen. I trust him on this one and always have Clyde back a day early. I'd cast spells while holding Clyde up to a full moon. He likes the moon. I can really feel his energy. Clyde has a wooden nose and a slight smirk on his strait mouth. The eyes are carved out. The rest of his figure is shaped by nature. I glue some small crystals for his eyes. The crystals keep falling out from time to time, and I just glue them back in. At one point I wrap a large quartz crystal around his forehead with thread. I think that this will make him more powerful. The thread covers his eyes. I did this after Grace had boiled him. I don't think he liked being boiled! I don't know whatever happens to Grace, as we never hear from her again. Both Fred's and my business start to pick up so our meetings pretty much come to an end.

Around August of that year, I have an extreme pain in my left eye area. I go to my family physician and she diagnoses pink eye and gives me some eye drops. I place cold compresses over my eye that night, as the pain is unbearable. The next morning I'm walking to my garden and notice the ground is wavy.

I close my right eye and see the ground in ocean waves and think, *What the fuck?*

I get dressed and speed to the ER.

While waiting in the emergency room of the Callahan Eye Foundation hospital I keep trying to read magazines with my left eye while closing my right eye. The writing is "whited out," a medical term that's later defined as white out! When I look at the words on the page they disappear and all I can see is white. The doctor comes in and begins the examination.

"You have a parasite in your eye," Dr. Albert says.

"A fucking parasite! What the fuck does that mean!" I say.

"We've never seen this in the United States, only in medical books. Have you been out of the country lately?" he says.

"No."

"Let me call the head of the department," he says while reaching for the phone on the wall.

"Great."

Different doctors begin to come in the exam room to view the parasite that's crawling around in my eye and leaving "tracks" on my macula. The creepy sickening feeling I'm getting from knowing that something is crawling around in my eye is almost too much to bear. They take me up to the doctors' offices and try to zap the little fucker with the laser. But every time they put the beam on it, it moves like a roach does when you turn the lights on. We'll have to give you a pesticide to kill it they tell me.

Over the next several days the Mintezol is making me sick as a roach! Every morning when I go to look at my garden the parasite has made more tracks. It's like I'm looking through sticks and branches. I can't stand it anymore and return to the doctor four days later.

"It's dead. It's just floating in your vitreous," Dr. Albert says.

"Thank God," I say.

After zapping it with the laser about twenty times just to make sure it doesn't move he says, "We can leave it in or we can surgically remove it and I'll do the surgery at no charge."

"Get that fucking thing out of my eye," I say.

I return to the doctor several days later to remove the patch over my eye. The medical books have a new entry. When the doctor removes the patch the vision in my left eye shows the office door sideways!

"What the fuck is this?" I ask.

"That will improve with time," he says. "There's really nothing else we can do. The macula is part of the brain and we don't have the technology to repair it."

I break down in heaving sobs as I cuss Clyde in silence.

Angry and shocked I spend the following week with an eye patch on going to meetings and cussing that fucking parasite.

"What's wrong with your eye?" people ask.

"I got a fucking parasite in it," I'd say.

"How did that happen?"

"I have no clue," I'd say, knowing deep inside that it was Clyde! His eyes falling out; the thread I wrapped the crystal around his head that covered his eyes . . . he didn't like being boiled! Later on I had a psychic reading that tells me that

**all my karma had been removed as a result of all this.**

# Chapter Ten

## *An Affair to Remember*

I've known Tracy for several years. When we met four years earlier, the electricity between us could light up New York City. But she was married and we went our separate ways until one night I walk into the Hoover meeting with my eye patch fully in place. I'm full of self-pity when she walks up to me after the meeting, electrified. She picks up a silver chip that night. She is extremely attractive, blond hair, great figure, and I can save her.

"I'm miserable and he's filed for divorce," she says.

I say, "Great! Let's go have some coffee and talk about it."

I begin to get out of the problem and into the solution of treating and healing my eye. A holistic practitioner friend of mine, Rama, suggests eyewash of Triphala powder. I boil the water and let the Triphala powder seep into the solution. I get an eyecup and begin soaking my eye every morning. I also meditate and imagine the tracks in my eye dissolving while chanting "Ohm" for thirty minutes. I do this for two months, every day. I also make positive affirmations, such as "My vision is getting better every day" and do Tibetan eye chart exercises.

"That's impossible!" Dr. Albert says a few months later. "The tracks are gone."

There's just a small semblance of a scar in the center of my macula. The Triphala powder and meditations worked! It's another entry in the medical books. (I find out later that my eye is hanging in the Callahan Eye Foundation Hospital!)

I take a cruise to celebrate.

I arrive back from the cruise and send Tracy a text, "Coffee?"

"Sure."

We'd meet for coffee over the next several weeks at Patton Creek. She calls me every morning, although she's still living with her husband. She has moved into a bedroom of her marital residence that's downstairs. I give her legal and marital advice since I'm an expert on both . . . and she complains about her situation and what an asshole her husband is. We develop a friendship. I give her foot massages while we discuss our lives.

She comes over to the house one night and I cook her dinner. I walk her out to her car, we kiss and I'm in love. Maybe the Chinese man said Tracy, not Teresa. Rationalization and justification is like masturbation. I'm only fucking myself.

"Why don't you just spend the night?" I say one evening as she's gathering her belongings to leave.

"Okay."

We make out for hours going no further than kissing. She looks like a model. Five foot six with shoulder-length color treated blond hair, brown eyes that sparkle with little flecks of light. She has manmade breasts that turn up a little at the end and a slim figure. She's currently suspended from nursing for stealing drugs.

She calls late one night complaining what *he* has done and I say, "Why don't you just come over?"

"Okay."

During one of the several hours long make out sessions she says, "I'm tired of this pseudo sex."

And I say, "Me too. Let's go smoke and talk about it."

We end up making love real slow that night.

The affair is on. The sex is phenomenal. When she leaves in the mornings my heart aches.

Thoughts trigger emotions. Emotions trigger thoughts. The thoughts of having found my true love keeps me high just like the crack had done before. Cuddling on the sofa our hearts synchronize as one. *She* is my true soul mate. We exchange "I love you" and "I miss you" constantly. We go to the beach together. The master bedroom shower is four times the size of a regular one. She asks me to come and wash her back in the shower. I undress while watching her naked body through the glass door. The scent of salt, sand, steam, and soap make me hard as a rock. I begin to wash her back as the hot steamy water pounds our bodies. I turn her around and our slippery embrace locks our bodies as one. Our hands are sliding all over each other. I take her leg and lift it as high is it will go and insert me in her wetness. Time stands still.

She tells me how great it is making love to her not the "sport fucking" she's accustomed to. The love affair's very intense and lasts about a month. We talk about our love constantly. We make love, not sex. She promises me we'll be together some day. She tells me she loves me more than I would ever know and even tells her boss that we're soul mates. She confides that she has always been crazy about me. She's afraid to be around me because she doesn't trust herself. She has *always* loved me and is excited and nervous to see me. She never liked anybody as much as she does me. We talk about our past relationships and feelings as I've never done with a woman before. She takes Ambien to sleep at night. When she comes over to spend the night I resist playing with her body after she falls asleep.

She won't get a sponsor so I try to help her find one. I tell her I'll be her temporary sponsor until she finds one. I give her numbers of other women in the program that offer to sponsor her. We work through the steps. We work step three and get on our knees while holding hands. We say the third step prayer.

I turn to her and we start making out and I say, "I don't normally do this with my sponsees."

"We can't continue this anymore," she says one night while we're having coffee.

"No more sex, no more hand holding, no more kissing, no more I love you, no more I miss you, no more love," she says, turning her love off like a faucet.

"No more!" I say, not yet realizing that I've done the same thing to Laura. What goes around comes around mother used to say.

Over the next several months I wait for her to come to her senses. We'd still meet for coffee and she'd come over to the house. I wanted that pseudo sex. I wanted that love back. I wanted us back like we were. Can't she see that we're meant to be! The unreturned love is killing me. She's cold as a snake.

"Don't call her. Don't text her. Don't email her," my grand sponsor, Dave, instructs.

"Get rid of her," my sponsor says that Christmas Eve.

"He can't do that," Dave says. "He's just going to keep picking the same women all over again. We'll fix that broken picker of yours."

"Thank God." I say knowing it's been broken for a long time.

Another self-examination and fourth step! I go home and start the examination:

What is being affected? Sex relations; emotional security; happiness. I'm swamped with guilt, self-loathing and melancholy. I'm hoping that our relationship returns to what it's like before she turned the faucet off. The more I try to control the outcome of the relationship, the less likely it's going to happen and the more frustrated I get. I'm still emotionally insecure and immature. I'm always attracted to women who have just as much "baggage" as I do. I try and save them by building up their self-esteem. My self-esteem is lost in the process. I'm playing God, again. If there were one hundred women lined up against a wall I'll pick the psycho and emotionally sickest one. I'm making demands on her to give me emotional security and happiness. When it gets to where I have that security and happiness *then* I will be happy. Then I'll feel OK about myself and with the world around me. This is an illusion. It's not real. The illusion has turned into an obsession. I'm full of fear of not getting what I want (demand) and my emotional security won't be met. I'm afraid that I'll never find another woman like her. I'm afraid that I won't have sex like I have with her anymore. It's still all about me! I put her first before God for my emotional security and happiness.

My pride and ego insist that I dominate Tracy, and I depend on her far too much. I have tried to manipulate her for my own willful desires for emotional security, happiness and sex. She resisted and I have hurt feelings along with a sense of persecution. Why is she doing this to me? She is doing exactly what she's supposed to do. She's just being who she is. As I redouble my efforts at control I continue to fail; my suffering becomes acute, constant, and turns into an obsession.

"Don't initiate anything. Let God, not you control the relationship," Dave instructs. He becomes my sponsor.

I need self-discipline. I have to force myself to quit checking the e-mail every thirty minutes. I have to quit saying I love you and I miss you. I'm only saying it to hear her say it back. I leave my phone at home because I think every ring is her calling. I have to quit masturbating every night while thinking of the sex we had. I'm only keeping the obsession burning, only throwing more wood on the fire. The only thing that's real is the obsession itself and everything, my thoughts, my wants, my needs, and desires are stemming from the obsession. I cancel plans in hopes that she will call to meet me. My demands and obsessions are opposing God's Grace.

I work Step Six; "Were entirely ready to have God remove all these defects of character." The defects of character are my demands and the obsession of trying to control the outcome of the relationship. I must have no reservations what-so-ever for God to remove the obsession from me and take action toward that goal. Am I entirely ready to rely on God? Am I ready to live with uncertainty and be comfortable with it? Hope appears when demands lessen. The desire for intimacy will always be there but am I willing to let time and God take control. I'm powerless and helpless about controlling outcomes of situations, relationships and everything else in life! I write this prayer: God help me. I don't know where it is going, but help me do the things I need to do to take me to where I need to go wherever it is going to take me.

I work Step Seven: "Humbly ask Him to remove my shortcomings." (Obsession) My goal in life comes out of trying to give not demanding that I receive. I must be willing to abandon everything and rely on God to relieve me of this obsession. I must rely on God's strength and intelligence, not John's. I must abandon the idea about how things are going to turn out. I don't know what will happen. I must look by faith, beyond the material things, where God resides. God's will leads me to peace, joy, and a surprise ending or unexpected result. My will leads to more chaos, drama and confusion! *He* will reveal what the outcome of any situation is and it is always better than what I could imagine. I must reach that level of peace and comfort beyond human understanding that the material world can neither give nor take away. I just do the work and God gives me that peace and comfort. By abandoning outcomes I will be given a working faith.

More instructions: go to Alanon; don't let up on any AA activities; no new sponsees. My sponsees become my sponsors. I begin helping set up meetings and making coffee. I get to the meetings early and put out chairs, tables and AA literature. I walk into a meeting and the chairman asks me to lead topics for discussion. I drive to a particular meeting place and suddenly change and go to a different meeting than I had originally planned. The meeting where I end up is the meeting where I hear exactly what I need or meet someone that I need to talk to. I stay after the meeting and help clean up. God puts me with people going through the same obsessions of trying to control outcomes of relationships. If I let up on my program activities nothing will get better and

I will get worse. I'm going to fifteen meetings a week. I stop expecting answers to questions that have no answers. I stop pursuing situations for which there are no solutions. I must live my way into sober thinking. God wants me to be with a woman who is better than I think I can have. I must stop pursuing women with low self-esteem and no emotional sobriety. I believe that God will provide me with someone better than I think I deserve. He will provide someone on His time and His manner. Happiness and emotional and financial security are gifts from God. Damn if I didn't keep forgetting this!

The battle between my ego and God begins. I'm trying to give up control over something I never had control of.

She gets divorced with my help (of course) and moves out of her marital residence. The attempts to change her are fruitless. I'm powerless over recapturing the love I thought we had. It's only my love for her that is sustained. I go to Alanon. I get back in the steps. I talk about it until I get tired of talking about it. Every thought I have is about her. What could I have done differently, what can I do differently and how can I make her realize the mistake she has made. I, I, I, me, me, me, I'm consumed with *me*!

"Call me," I say as she is leaving my house for the last time.

"What?" She says with a blank, emotionless stare in her eyes.

That's the last time I saw her and knew it was over. It's January twelfth, two thousand seven. She dies from an overdose of heroin in two thousand eighteen.

# Chapter Eleven

## *The Awakening*

*"Listen.*
*The words to the next song you hear. The*
*information in the next article you read. The story*
*line of the next movie you watch. The chance*
*utterance of the next person you meet; or the*
*whisper of the next river; the next ocean; the next*
*breeze that caresses your ear. All these devices are*
*Mine-All these avenues are open to me. I will speak*
*to you if you will listen. I will come to you if you*
*invite me. I will show you then that I have always*
*been there. All ways."*
-Neale Donald Walsh, Conversations With God,
Part 1

I continue to meet with Dave and earnestly
work back through the steps. The only reality is

the obsession itself. My thoughts, my wants, my desires, and needs are all an illusion. I'd been demanding that Tracy give me back the intimacy we had before. It's the basic need for an intimate relationship with another human being that I always long for, except for an alcoholic like me, it gets taken to the extreme and is always based on how they look and not their character.

I turn to the only Source I knew. I pray on my knees all through the day. I begin meditating on my chakras for at least an hour every morning. Escape into the soothing waters and scent of lavender provides the closeness of my Creator. I receive messages as I come out of the meditative states. A loud voice in my head overcomes all thoughts when God says:

"Nothing can thwart God's will. What you do to the least of them you do to Me."

I know this Voice does not come from me. I had never used the word "thwart" before and have no idea what it means. I look up the definition: thwart: To block or defeat. Shit, that's exactly what I'm doing. God apparently does not want me to be with Tracy. This is the beginning of my second surrender.

I finish my meditation and God gives me prayers to repeat. I use them until they don't work anymore and then He gives me another. I write them down:

"God, let my mind be Your Mind."

"I am yours, God. John."

"I am yours, John. God."

"All power is of God. What is not of Him has no power to do anything."

I start coming up with my own prayers:

*God give me Your strength to handle all my problems.*

*God, give me patience, kindness tolerance and love for Tracy.*

*God grant me peace knowing that Your will, not mine be done.*

*God, give me the willingness to become willing to let go of John absolutely.*

*God, grant Tracy peace, happiness and serenity.*

Then He gives me more:

*I want you to stay in My world.*

*Don't forget Me.*

I start step eleven:

*"Sought through prayer and meditation to improve our conscious contact with God as we understood Him."*- Alcoholics Anonymous

I realize I'm trying to solve the problem of emotional security by relying on another human being and not God. I get a "shit eating" grin for longer periods.

God says, "Keep praying until you get peace." I follow His instructions and get peace and glimpses of God's kingdom.

"There is a direct linkage among self-examination, meditation and prayer. Taken separately, these practices can bring much relief and benefit. But when they are logically related and interwoven, the result is an unshakeable foundation for life. Now and then we may be granted a glimpse of that ultimate reality which is God's kingdom." -Twelve Steps and Twelve Traditions.

That "glimpse of God's kingdom" is a feeling of love, joy, and peace. It's not a place but is beyond this world of human understanding. By living the program, God grants this to me. Sometimes I think I can generate this feeling, but that is trying to control the outcome. It's a process of self-examination, meditation, and prayer. God grants these gifts of His kingdom.

I discover further that I think I can control and manipulate women with low self-esteem by being demanding or gracious as the case may be. I'm not "good enough" for non-alcoholic women or so I think. A woman who feels good about her self intimidates me. Hell, there's nothing to work with! I am good enough! I do have a lot to offer! I've got a lot of work to do on myself.

My heart glows with joy and that shit eating grin starts to last all day. Other alcoholics need rides to meetings. I get new sponsees. I have gratitude and thank God all during the day.

I stop working steps with Dave at Step Eleven. God continues to send me messages and says to just watch the thoughts that go through your head.

Don't attach them to any emotion. They are just thoughts, like clouds floating by.

The words in "How it Works" take on a new meaning. "The results were nil until we let go absolutely." "Half-measures availed us nothing." The more I surrender self the more peace and joy I get. I'm surrendering self by working the program. I suddenly realize that the purpose of the whole affair with Tracy is to establish a relationship with my Creator I've never had before. I begin to thank Tracy for showing John to himself! I see why people relapse. They're not willing to do the work that is necessary to maintain their sobriety. Not many people make it past the five-year mark. I pick up my six-year chip. It's March twenty fourth, two thousand seven.

"I'm not a victim of others, but rather a victim of my expectations, choices and dishonesty. When I expect others to be what I want them to be and not who they are, they fail to meet my expectations and I'm hurt. When my choices are based on self-centeredness I'm lonely and distrustful". *As Bill Sees It.* I have to watch my motives. I need to make sure that whatever it is I am doing, it's not to make John feel better about himself.

I go to the bookstore and buy *The Power of Now* by Eckhart Tolle. I study it. Then I live it by imagining a separate part of myself who becomes the "observer" or the "watcher" of my thoughts. There are my thoughts. Then there's the observer who watches my thoughts. I call this observer Little John. When the obsessive thoughts flare up I say, "Come here Little John and watch these thoughts." Little John comes and sits next to me and without judgment watches my thoughts. The obsession begins to evaporate.

"You've got to watch this movie Dad," Johnny says.

"What movie?" I say still reeling from the breakup.

"What the Bleep Do We Know?"

"What's it about?"

"Just watch it."

Quantum physics for dummies, synchronicity and the role consciousness plays in your life are the themes. I live in a "light" based universe. Everything is light and within that light is an intelligence or God. If I cut a piece of wood and chop it up into its smallest pieces, down to an atom, and even further beyond the atom there exists a flickering light. Then if I chop a part of my body and break it down into its smallest pieces beyond the atom and even further there exists a flickering light! I am the light! I begin to wake up from a dream. Several days later I go to the Galleria mall. I walk into the food court and there are hundreds of high school children dressed in black pants and white shirts eating lunch. Time begins to slow down. My body is moving in slow motion. Everything is surreal. Out of the corner of my eye

I notice two boys throwing a superball back and forth. In perfect stride walking in slow motion my left hand rises up to my shoulder. I catch the ball one of the boy's has missed. With an unbelievable look on their faces, I throw the ball back to them. The whole event is synchronized perfectly. I look at them and they look at me like who is this guy?

A "circle" appears in my front yard. It's approximately six to eight feet in diameter. I can sense energy coming from it. I take pictures at night and the camera reveals orbs and fluxes of energy emanating from the circle. I can't see the vortex of energy nor the orbs with my naked eye. The infrared vision of the camera picks up this energy flux and the orbs. The orbs are all different sizes and multicolored. They are floating out of the circle and all around my yard. I research orbs wondering what they are. They seem to be an otherworldly consciousness or intelligence. Some armchair critics explain them away as dust specks on the camera lens. They're too beautiful and symmetrical to be dust and they move!

I'm consumed with reading all kinds of spiritual literature, books, Internet articles and blogs on MySpace. I start my own blog. A lot of the articles I'm reading mention *A Course in Miracles. (The Course)* The introduction says, "This is a course in miracles. It is a required course. Only the time you take it is voluntary.

Free will does not mean that you can establish the curriculum. It means only that you can elect what you want to take at a given time. The course does not aim at teaching the meaning of love, for that is beyond what can be taught. It does aim, however, at removing the blocks to the awareness of love's presence, which is your natural inheritance. The opposite of love is fear, but what is all-encompassing can have no opposite." This course can be summed up very simply in this way:
"Nothing real can be threatened.
Nothing unreal exists.
Herein lies the peace of God."
I remember I have that book. I'd bought the book about three years prior and couldn't comprehend it so I put it on the bookshelf. It's about the destruction of the ego and forgiveness. There is "the book" and then there are "lessons" that you take one per day for 365 days. It's just the course I need. I can understand it now! I start the lessons in earnest. The introduction to the workbook says; "The workbook is divided into two main sections, the first dealing with the undoing of the way you see now, and the second with the acquisition of true perception." (Programming, conditioning and love respectively). "The purpose is to train your mind in a systematic way to a different perception of everyone and everything in the world." It's April twenty fourth, two thousand seven.

Over the next three months, I come to a new level of existence or being. I begin the process of surrendering self (ego). I further awaken to The Kingdom of God. Life becomes surreal. A friend, Rachel, informs me that Wayne Dyer is coming to Birmingham. I'd been reading his books for years. I'd just finished reading *Manifest Your Destiny*. I arrive at the location where he is to appear. I bring his book so he can sign it. When I meet him he sits down right next to me. The intensity I feel while he concentrates on listening to someone else talk leaves a high pitch ringing in my ear. I'm literally "high" from his energy for two weeks afterward. I talk to him about my recent awakening and I tell him I'm reading Eckert Tolle's book.

He says, "I love him; we believe he's a walk-in." A walk-in is a spirit that "walks in" to your body by a previous soul agreement before you come to Earth. Your spirit walks out and the "new" spirit walks in.

It's one of the greatest events in my life! He autographs his book, "John, to a life without limits! Love Wayne Dyer." I later have it framed.

He says, "That's my favorite book; I channeled the whole thing."

I have spiritual experiences one after the other. I meditate by bringing energy into my chakras for an hour a day. I experience more joy, peace, happiness, and serenity than I ever had. I live what I've been reading about all my life.

I help organize a golf event for Focus on Recovery. It's a women's halfway house in Hoover. I hear that James Redfield, author of *The Celestine Prophecy, The Secret of Shambhala, The Tenth Insight, The Twelfth Insight* and many others, will be playing in the event. The manager of Focus, Rachel, teams me with James and we play in the tournament together and ride in the same golf cart! Also on the team is Larry Miller, author of *Holographic Golf: Uniting the Mind and Body to Improve Your Game.* After the event I get James's autograph and he writes, "To John, You really saved the team with those birdies! Best Always, James Redfield." I wait in anticipation to see what God will show me next. I perceive the world in a new light.

The next several months I continue bringing energy into my chakras during my morning meditations. At first I'm bringing the energy in through the third eye chakra. Then I place a clear quartz crystal over the individual chakra and the chakra itself draws the energy in. At first the chakras just need energy. Then they start expanding into the room and enveloping the house. Next they burst with color streaming out of the windows, doors, and cracks of the house out into the universe. Sometimes it's as if the chakras are sending out electrical lines and expanding as big as the earth. It's an incredible time, mystical and magic. There seems to be no end or depth to it.

*The Course* describes how thoughts are mostly attack thoughts. I either attack others by judging them or I am attacking myself by judging me. I perceive that other people are attacking me by their words. People aren't attacking me; they're just being who they are. Or they don't feel good about themselves and project that on to another person. I slowly let go of guilt (self-attack) and ego (attacking others). My thoughts are based on previous experiences or prior programming and conditioning. They neither are real nor based on who the person or thing really is.

My son Johnny teaches me how to really "see." I focus on a tree and see it glow. I come to believe that everything is God and He glows! To see the aura of the tree I focus my eyes on just one part of it like a branch or leaf. I don't move my eye or blink. I continue to hold my gaze. After a few seconds I see a white glow emanating from around the tree and people, too.

During my chakra meditation one morning, the light, colors, and energy from the chakras are coming out of all openings of my body, even the pores. After the meditation, God says, "Bring my children home." Home to me is Heaven on Earth. I need to help show people by example, Who they really are, an eternal being having a human experience. I notice if I concentrate on listening and placing my entire attention on a person's body, especially the head, I can see a luminous glow emanating from his or her body. It's really out of this world . . . I feel at one with God and all living things. I'm not special. God talks to everybody all the time; the question is do I listen? Do I stay in the dark (asleep) or do I awaken to Gods kingdom, here and now in the present.

I'm still receiving messages from God and He gives me a message, "Everybody wants to be loved, so love everybody!" During one meditation the top three chakras start to "spin" and I get an incredible feeling of joy in my heart area.

I find a meditation called the Violet Flame Meditation. After I do this I feel very light and wonderful! The author says the violet flame is a powerful tool anyone can use in meditation. It helps release negative karma, raise your consciousness awareness, the frequency of your vibration, and accelerate your spiritual growth. Energy can't be erased but it can be changed, transmuting negative into positive, darkness into light. This allows me to make the choices I feel negatively about and transmute them into positive, while also changing my emotional experience. Physically, the violet flame releases emotions and pent up energy within that make me vulnerable to illness and disease.

The violet flame in meditation uses a combination of affirming thoughts and visualization. Once centered, (bring all of me into the center of my being) I begin by surrounding myself with white-and-blue protective energy. (I don't need any "protection" while I go into this powerful spiritual state because I am already a powerful spiritual being.) I can however, if it makes me more comfortable. Then I repeat thoughts such as "I am cleansed and purified by the violet flame." "I am the light." "I am the truth." I picture a huge bonfire before me, its immensity making me feel small beside it, and marvel as the colors flicker between purple, violet, and bright pink. I sense its warmth while noticing that it will not burn me. I step into the flame, letting it surround me entirely while also filling the spaces in my body, thoughts, even the cells and molecules within me. Once there, I focus on the positive things I'd like to create in my life. Then I can spread the flame out from where I am to the world around me while repeating, "This house is cleansed and purified by the violet flame." "This city is cleansed and purified by the violet flame." I visualize the violet flame in the midst of the scenes as they unfold in my mind. I may want to ask that the power of the flame be multiplied to assist those in need.

When I have finished my meditation, I try to be sure to close with gratitude. The violet flame is a powerful tool that should be used consciously and with intent. It is always a good idea when finished with any spiritual practice to give thanks as this creates closure. Saints and adepts throughout the ages have known how to use the violet flame, but it is available for all to use to raise our awareness and, eventually, that of all mankind. -Unknown Source

It is so true how often I either belittle myself, i.e. I think I'm not good enough or I am ruler of the world! All of these illusions are part of the egoist mind, which have no basis in reality-a self-imposed narcissistic illusion. We're all parts of the whole (holy) of God and no one is neither greater than nor less than the other. We're all the same and of equal importance in God's kingdom. Religions want to make me believe (make believe) that I must go through them to "get to heaven." Religion destroys spirituality, government destroys freedom, and education destroys individuality. There is no getting to heaven. I'm already there in this holy moment. It's a state of mind.

While I'm doing the violet flame exercise one morning, (and during a lot of the other exercise periods) I can feel God's presence in my heart. His presence is the feeling of joy in my heart that makes it seem like it is glowing. When I realize that everything is holy and everything is God, a great feeling of awe, compassion, and gratitude for life comes over me. I try and not take life for granted and see the holiness in everything. When I read one of *The Course's* morning lessons, I immediately break down crying realizing how selfish I've been all my life. When I'm able to see God in everyone and bless him or her as a part of me, I discover the true meaning of unconditional love. I can only imagine what kind of world that would be if everyone did the same. Everyone is my teacher. What I see in them I see in me. What I don't like in them is a part of me I don't like.

I feel that my ego is trying to make me let up on *The Course* as it knows its end is near. I feel that I must continue to practice the lessons because I do not want to live like I have in the past with fear, judgment, and incessant chattering of the ego. The only moment is the holy instant of now. This is where the creator resides, not in the past or the future, only in the moment. This is why it is called the present. It is God's gift to all. My goal is to bring into alignment my ego, human self, with my eternal God self. It's simple but not easy. It takes a persistent and consistent effort to recognize and replace my thoughts, words, and actions.

I have no beliefs, only perceptions that change based on the state of mind I'm in at the time the belief is formed from experience. Belief is defined as an opinion or conviction, principle or idea accepted as true. A belief is only a thought repeated over and over again. To believe is to have confidence in the truth (*your truth*) of the existence or reliability of something, although without absolute proof that one is right in doing so. Perception is the apprehending by means of the senses or of the mind. (Which is where?) Perceiving is cognition, understanding; to become aware of; to know, from the Latin, to lay hold of.

In childhood (and today) my beliefs were (are) influenced by my parents, media, teachers, government, religions, friends, etc. (what they believe or want you to believe). For instance, I was taught in elementary school and college that oil came from dead dinosaurs and that we would eventual run out! Remember Sinclair Oil with the dinosaur on the sign? Fossil fuels? Such bullshit! The earth makes oil and is abundant, for instance, see abiotic oil. My mind was (and is) a sponge, soaking up thousands of bits of information visually and sublimely. The most sophisticated super computer in the Universe, sorting, analyzing, storing, deleting, and recording everything constantly. The past conditioning and programming are constantly running in the background running like a loop on a video recording. Most of my thoughts are not my own nor original! My goal is to sort through the menagerie of conditioning and programming, delete the ones that do not serve me, move them to the trash bin and empty them. My ultimate goal is to delete the thoughts that are contrary to unconditional love: to love all creation without condition or judgment.

One of the lessons in *The Course* says, "The purpose of today's exercises is to begin to instill in you a sense that you have dominion over all things because of what you are."

"Your holiness reverses all the laws of the world. It is beyond every restriction of time, space, distance, and limits of any kind. Your holiness is totally unlimited in its power because it establishes you as a Son of God, at one with the Mind of his Creator."

"If you are holy, so is everything God created. You are holy because all things He created are holy. And all things He created are holy because you are." *A Course in Miracles*

I really have trouble with this lesson. My ego wants to think "I" am all-powerful. The power comes from God, The Creator of Words; this Universal intelligence not me. Who keeps me breathing at night? How does my heart beat and the trillions of chemical reactions that go on in my body every second? It has to come from love, compassion, and understanding, not from the various forms of the egoist, delusional mind! I attempt this lesson and there is a great sense of resistance. I realize this is due to nothing but fear of moving toward the light and the death of ego. My ego wants to make me believe that I can't do this or that I am not a holy Son of God, but in reality it (ego) fears its own loss of power over me. As I'm reading the lesson this morning a car drives by playing "Stairway to Heaven" at the same time I'm reading the part about how meaningless my fears are. It strikes me how funny this is. I realize that I'm "practicing" these lessons. It's an attempt to reach the light. My ego wants me to attack myself and tell me that I can't do this course.

After practicing the lesson all day I believe it. I realize how much of my thoughts have been of the ego. It is extremely powerful but is not more powerful than God. I love myself more than I ever have and I try to extend this to others. I become grateful for the path I'm on and become determined to be rid of my egoism or at least recognize it for what it is.

During one of my violet flame meditations, I step out of the flame while giving thanks. In my mind's eye I look up and angels surround me. I feel the presence of Gabriel. I'm not exactly sure who she is but I research Angels. The Angels fill me with light through the top of my head. They then hug me and I thank God.

My father has given us his old car and I gave it to Johnny. He takes the car to visit his cousin, Ashley, in Ft. Lauderdale. The car breaks down and he just leaves it somewhere in between. I had several items stolen out of my yard: a motorcycle, tools, a well-seasoned grill, and an attempt to steal my riding lawnmower. By staying steadfast to the Course, I manage to keep my peace, happiness, and joy throughout these ordeals. I do get angry several times, but by repeating *The Course* lessons over and over in my head, the peace and joy returns rather quickly. *The Course* literally transforms my thinking, feeling, and emotional state. My ego wants to blame, judge, criticize, surmise, at nauseam. I'm able to recognize when it (ego) comes up and immediately able to bring myself back to the present moment.

I become friends with a woman on MySpace and ask her about my awakening and what is going on. I write her and say,
June eleventh, two thousand seven-three thirty-three p.m. (Note the synchronistic time).

"I have to talk to somebody! I am an attorney in Birmingham specializing in criminal defense, personal injury and divorce. (Whew!) I have been reading everybody's bulletins and seeing all my friends awakening and I feel a change not only in the way we will think, but also a planetary shift? My son is obsessed with God and the Light as well as me and I have had no energy to work. The only energy is to talk with other conscious people and read spiritual information. My son is "seeing" an actual earth turning "inside out" and my lesson yesterday from "A Course in Miracles" talked about how we were seeing everything upside down and our thoughts are backwards. Everyone thinks

he needs to be committed, but I can see some truth in what he is thinking and saying. I feel this change is going to happen soon, but I know it is only in the mind of God. Thanks for listening and I feel much better now! Thank you so much for all the knowledge and love and light you have been giving me. Any thoughts on the matter would be enlightening!"
John
She writes me back and says,
John:

"Your son is not crazy. Neither are you and neither am I. That's the good news. I've known for quite some time that the earth is *already* anchored in the fifth dimension. You did not? That's where this ascension process comes in. We must transform ourselves through love in order to move with mother earth. She's *already* there . . . think about that . . . your lesson is right when it suggested we were seeing everything upside down and our thoughts are backwards . . . think about that . . . people who *are no*t familiar with the light and ascension, etc., are going to have a very rude awakening as this whole process continues. But we must not judge them or get upset when they are judging us, only unconditional love for all will get you through this. :) The ones who are still asleep (not ascending) are the ones who are seeing everything upside down and their thoughts are backwards, it's the way we use to think too.

Remember? And now that you are waking up, it's no wonder you don't want to go work and do the same ole same ole, you are actually feeling how *extremely* important it is to not focus on anything right now except with your spirituality and ascension and learning and talking to others on your same path. Nothing is what it seems John . . . at all, but relax, I'm going to give you a little advice that I follow. With *everything* and *anything* you do from now on, before you act or talk, or even think, asks yourself one question . . . *what would love do now*?"

love,

dee**

The Sumarian Texts speak of the Annunaki, the Gnostic Gospels speak of the Archons. Religious texts write about devils and demons. Who is in control and corrupting the corruptible?

Johnny tells me a few years earlier that he's gay and that he's known this since he was twelve but was afraid to tell me. I tell him I love him anyway no matter what, unconditionally. I come home from work and he's all so fucked up on pain pills. It makes me angry and my first sponsor wants to come over and throw him out of the house. I don't have the guts to do it. *The Course* lessons stress forgiveness and controlling or changing your thoughts. If I can't control or change my thoughts then who can? I truly forgive him for being fucked up all the time and I realize the reason I'm angry with him is because I'm seeing myself. When I accept him for who he is and not for whom I think he should be, he decides to move out! I'm learning the lessons of unconditional love and true forgiveness. I'm becoming free of myself. I'm not worrying about the future or regretting the past and I'm living more in the moment. Everything else is really an illusion. It exists only in my mind. My perception shifts even more and I feel the attack thoughts diminishing.  I accept people, places, and things as they are not as I think they should be.  I accept creation as it is, not the way John thinks it should be.

# Chapter Twelve

## *Visions & Auras*

I go to Hilton Head for the Fourth of July. It's time for the "Fire the Grid" (the Grid is the network of energy surrounding the earth) worldwide event set for July seven, two thousand seven. All across the world people meditate for an hour synchronized at the same time and send love to Mother Earth. One of the ways suggested by the project is to connect with the earth while embracing a tree for an hour, sending thoughts of love down through the ground into her center. Hilton Head is the perfect place. It's man and nature united. The houses and buildings are incorporated into the environment. The trees and native plants are kept and the architecture is built around them, unlike most cities where everything is mowed down and replaced with concrete and steel. I can actually "feel" the electric energy. It's like the electric energy I feel during a lightning storm. During the event at the synchronized time, I find a nice big tree and wrap my arms around her for an hour sending love, peace, and selfishness into the earth. I release all my burdens and when it's over I feel more connected to the earth and to nature. I can actually feel the grid become energized. I realize that the earth provides me with an abundance of food, air and water. If it wasn't for Mother Earth, I can't live. I think most people have lost their connection with the earth.

I see the numbers eleven-eleven everywhere. I wake up at night; look at the clock and its eleven-eleven, or three thirty-three or four forty-four. I don't know what this means so I research it and discover eleven-eleven is a wake-up call from my "higher self." It means that it's time for me to wake up from the illusion of "reality." I quit living in the illusion; it's not real. The only reality is heaven and the spirit world. *This* is my home, not my body, my money, my homes or my jobs. Any time I see a synchronistic number it means I'm on the right path, thinking the right thought or saying the right word. When I see a synchronistic number I ask myself, what am I thinking when I see it. No matter what anyone says, everyone is right, according to *them*. What is right for me is based on *my* lifetime of programming, conditioning, research, influences, experiences, etc. Therefore, all argument is futile because you are trying to convince someone that your right is better than their right.

I have my aura photograph taken. The aura program analyzes the results and the reading is perfectly in sync with the experiences I'm having. It reads:

CROWN (COSMIC CONNECTION):

The crown chakra summarizes your total energy state. When we are experiencing changes, colors in our energy field will fluctuate wildly. However, colors in the crown chakra will reflect our resonant color.

AQUAMARINE CROWN:

You have a compassionate, sensitive, and peaceful nature, and wish for your relationship's to be easy and flowing. You are fully aware of how to encourage and nurture others with firmness and affection. With your natural ability to counsel others, you may find yourself attracted to a partner with vibrant golden tones whose fiery and spunky personality responds well to the parent within your spirit, which may occasionally cause some conflicts in your otherwise peaceful existence. With your encouragement, such a person may instantly take to you as a sensitive and caring confidant who they can trust to tame their secret desire for artistic freedom. You may also find that a partner with whom you share similar blue or green tones will be equally as attractive to you. If you choose a partner with your tones you will likely both nurture each other's sunny sides while providing a caring and compassionate environment in which your relationship will grow.

**VIOLET THIRD EYE (EXPERIENCE):**

The color seen over your brow is what you now experience for yourself. It's the color that would best describe your spiritual vision.

**RED THIRD EYE:**

Right now you are experiencing a time of challenge with an action packed schedule barely leaving you time to breathe, let alone sleep. You have a lot to do, and you have the energy and power to move mountains at this point in your life. You may find yourself acting as a dynamic leader, or find yourself in the limelight, or the center of attention. You are definitely being noticed. You have so much energy you sometimes don't know what to do with it. You may exhaust the people around you with your incredible enthusiasm. (I go to meetings and people comment on my shit-eating grin. They want what I have. I'm leading topic discussions and people talk about them for weeks).

**LEFT SIDE (FUTURE):**

The color on the left side is normally the vibration coming into your being. The closer it is to you the sooner it will be felt: perhaps within a few moments, hours or as long as a few months.

**TURQUOISE LEFT:**

Blue is the color of communication and intuition while green is the color of change. A blue-green, then, indicates new learning. Blue also signifies the ability to listen and receive information. Expect to be entering a time of peaceful receptivity when you will be able to learn many new things. (I soon start my studies of metaphysics).

VIOLET RIGHT:

The world cannot help but notice your glorious inner light. Your aura shines and radiates outward towards others with loving, healing energy. You put the highest vibrational frequency out into the world. Violet symbolizes magic, mysticism, and visionary capacity and also indicates a person who is profoundly insightful and keenly aware of their spiritual path. You have the ability to be a charismatic spiritual leader.

THROAT (COMMUNICATION):

The color of the throat chakra is traditionally the energy being expressed. It reflects the vibrational frequency most likely seen or felt by others around you. Many times your friends will think this is the energy that you are made of. However, it is the energy you are putting out into the world.

ORANGE THROAT:

You can't help expressing yourself creatively. Your voice is your instrument. You may enjoy singing, acting, telling jokes, and stories, or just chatting with friends. People find you a lively and entertaining companion. You are warm, outgoing, and sociable. (When I talk, everyone turns around to listen, my voice vibrates frequency).

**HEART (EMPATHY):**

The color on the heart chakra center represents your vibration of connection, affinity, compassion and empathy. How you feel about yourself and others is reflected here. If you feel intense passion for someone or something the energy in this center will be very strong.

**LAVENDER HEART:**

You glow with a magical and mysterious inner light. There's something different about you. You have a "sixth sense," and a strong connection with the divine. You live by faith and you believe in miracles. Always seeming to be in the right place at the right time, you are magically guided by a higher power. You work to heal yourself and others. You are always seeing the bigger picture and yourself reflected in the cosmos. The mundane details of life often bore you. Paying the bills seems far less important than meditating daily or writing down your visions from dreams or pondering your favorite current fantasy. You exist in another world far more beautiful and humane than the one in which everyone else lives. (At meetings people comment on how blissful I am. They ask me how I'm feeling and I say, "Absolutely incredible! I'm exploding into a million pieces of joy.").

## SOLAR PLEXUS (POWER):

The color on the solar plexus is normally the center vibration of your being. The Solar Plexus is associated with power or wealth, and is called the "money pot" by the Hindus. This is the center of self-esteem and ego.

## BLUE-WHITE SOLAR PLEXUS:

Blue is the color of peace, meditation, intuition, and tranquility and white is the color of spirituality. This mixture of blue and white indicates that you are now creating experiences of intense beauty, harmony, inner peace, and oneness with the divine. A beautiful healing energy spirals from your center to those around you. You may be able to act as a clear conduit for spiritual healing vibrations to flow through you to heal yourself and others. You are probably working on developing a close connection with the Creator through some kind of spiritual practice or artistic pursuit. (I've been meditating, praying, working the Course in Miracles and practicing mental/occult exercises).

## SEX (CREATIVITY):

This energy center of the body is about playfulness, sociability, and one's emotional life. It is a profound source of creativity, joy and pleasure that is nurturing, healing and bonding, and sexuality in adults. Many religions consider sex sinful. This belief can create a source of guilt, fear, and shame. When the energy in this area is balanced, the person will probably have a healthy positive attitude toward basic love. The sexual center is the position from which one reaches out, expands and relates to others. (I have a lot of guilt for using women my entire life).

**BLUE-WHITE SEX:**

"Peace loving" and "healing" best describe how you relate to others at this point in your life. You are a natural, clear conduit for spiritual healing energy. This light colored blue indicates you are in a regenerative, restful phase, and may be taking "time out" from sexual and romantic liaisons. If you are in a relationship, this is probably a time you are both focusing on friendship, companionship, and spiritual growth. In the blue-white sex chakra we see that you may find yourself gently encouraging and nurturing others. Presently, your highest goals are to achieve complete inner peace and to develop harmonious communication with others. You are definitely a "giver." (I'm at a place where I'm taking a break from dating concentrating instead on my spiritual development. I have reached that place of peace and joy that the world can neither give, nor take away).

**ROOT (GROUNDING):**

The color in the area of the root chakra is traditionally the energy of the physical plane and material reality. People with strong energy in this center usually have a red color and possess good survival skills. This is also the center of manifestation. If you are trying to succeed in the world either by making more money, establishing a business, or accumulating possessions, you will be focusing your energy here. This is also the place from which passion flows. It is the source of power and ego development.

LAVENDER ROOT:

You put out the highest vibrational frequency into the world. White represents spirituality and intense healing while violet symbolizes magic, mysticism, and visionary capacity. A combination of these two colors indicates a person who is profoundly magical and keenly aware of their spiritual path. Somehow you have managed to transcend the physical plane, because you easily negotiate your worldly affairs without worry, stress, or effort. Others wonder how you accomplish things so easily. You just let everything flow and everything gets done. (I'm in the "river" of life. I surrendered completely and allow the stream to carry me rather than continue to swim upstream). -WinAura Systems. (Company that makes the aura machine).

I find a website www.jamesclairlewis.com and begin a course in meditations that centers on metaphysical/occult exercises wherein certain mantras are repeated in the energy centers of the body. These are exercises that have been kept secret by the mystery schools for thousands of years as he describes it. I complete a year of this practice and decide to join The Brotherhood of the White Temple: "The Brotherhood" was formed in 1930 by Dr. Doreal as a channel for bringing the Ancient Wisdom to mankind. He has studied the Kabbala of the Hebrews, Christian Mysticism, Yoga and all other branches of the Ancient Wisdom. His teachings have reached students in all parts of the world: Over one million books and pamphlets written by Dr. Doreal have been distributed so that your instruction is directly from him. He carefully watches your progress and from time to time gives the individual instruction so necessary for progress." -*The Brotherhood of the White Temple.* They send me one lesson per week and I practice them for a week. They get harder and more complicated as time passes. I pronounce certain mantras in certain energy centers of the body. I do yoga exercises and practice rituals with candles. I'm working my job and attempting to do the lessons in a timely manner until, finally, after six months I'm worn out, overwhelmed, and say fuck it. (I'm really trying to control the outcome of my spiritual growth).

# Chapter Thirteen

## *This Shit is Real*

I have a client in drug court one morning; it's around January of two thousand eight and I see Tracy sitting in the courtroom. Shit, my heart jumps out of my chest. I've heard nothing from her since she left my house that night.

"I had no business having an affair with you," I say.

"Let's go smoke." She says as we walk outside. She tells me how she got arrested for forging scripts and is now in drug court.

This explains everything as she had been taking Lortab the entire time we were together.

I can't get enough of spirituality. In April of two thousand eight, I go to "Stargate Metaphysics" in Nashville and meet William Henry, an investigative mythologist, author, and radio host. I make him a wand at the urging of my "spirit guides." William is a phenomenal, down to earth human being with a wealth of knowledge and understanding of the workings of the universe, symbolism, and ancient cultures. We learn about stargates, secrets of enlightenment, Egyptian technologies, and cosmic freedom. The energy is electric. We tour Nashville's Parthenon that is an exact replica of the one in Greece. Within the complex there is the statute of Athena, the Greek goddess of wisdom. Photographs of her show orbs surrounding her.

We walk Centennial Park that is constructed to resemble a "rod." There are seven areas incorporated into the layout to represent the seven chakras! The Gardens of Babylon flank one side of the park! William joins me for breakfast one morning and we discuss my awakening.

In June, I attend the first Dreamland Festival and meet Ann and Whitley Strieber, Jim Marrs and Linda Moulton Howe. We all enjoy a guided "Crop Circle Meditation" led by Whitley.

The crop circle meditation brings me joy. I relax and notice my breath and continue to relax all the muscles in my body from the top of the head down into the feet as before. Now I imagine being in the center of a crop circle I have seen or just make one up. I keep the image of the circle in my mind and either by myself, a group or with someone I choose to be there with me, I begin to dance. I dance as long as my mind can hold it. I take this image with me anywhere and return to it in times of emotional distress. -*Whitley Strieber's Crop Meditation*

I hear that Wayne Dyer is coming to Atlanta and I convince several people including his daughter, Sommer, to go. I especially want her to go because she can get us in free! We arrive at the seminar and wait for Wayne. His entourage arrives and we follow them into the auditorium where we all have front row seats reserved. He tells stories just as incredible as his books. His theme is forgiveness. Sommer's older sister, Skye is there. Skye looks at Sommer and makes an announcement how she has forgiven Sommer. The whole audience starts crying.

Wayne cries, wipes his tears, and holds out his handkerchief and says, "Anybody want this, you can sell it on E-Bay!"

Sommer turns to me and says, "John, none of this could have happened if you hadn't convinced me to come."

Marianne Williamson comes to Atlanta. Some friends, Ginny, Lyndsey and I go to her seminar. I make Marianne a wand to give her. The wands have their own consciousness and it can't wait to be with her. Lyndsey holds the wand all the way there. Our minds are synchronized during the two and one-half hour drive. I'd think a thought and one of the girls says it. I say something and one of them says, "I was just thinking about that."

Synchronicity happens faster than the speed of light! I think a thought and Marianne says it. I had just read her book, *Everyday Grace* that she signed, "For John, Thank you for the gift, With Love, Marianne Williamson." It's the beginning of an awakening for Lyndsey.

Dannion Brinkley comes to Birmingham and my friend Carol and I go see him at Unity Church. Dannion is the author of *Saved by the Light*. He describes a near death experience where he's struck by lightning. He's pronounced dead and taken to the morgue. He recalls floating above his body and then going through a tunnel of light. He then "arrives" to the other side and stands before a group of light beings. They communicate with him. He is shown what he calls a "panoramic life review" where he observes all the people that he has interacted with during his lifetime. The perspective is from *their* viewpoint and how he affected *them*, good and bad. There is no judgment, just how he had affected them. The meaning of "do unto others" takes on a whole new meaning for me. That night we attend a dinner where James Redfield (Red, as Dannion calls him) makes an appearance. After the dinner, Carol and I are able to talk with James. We discuss Carol and my awakening briefly and he tells us he's writing *The Twelfth Insight*. It's about living the Ten Insights, synchronicity and coming from unconditional love. It's an honor for me to be so personal with these great spiritual teachers.

We start a meditation group. I make everybody wand's and we meet once a week. I lead the meditations. We do the chakra meditation, the violet flame, and whatever else I had learned or read about during the previous week. We'd send love to Mother Earth and bathe her in the violet flame. We can feel Her love for us. One of the girls, Cynthia, suggests that I sell my wands. I set up shop in one of the bedrooms in my house and get a copyright on the name "ascension wand." I design a web site and began making wands.

I instruct people how to use the wands using the knowledge I gain in my studies of the law of attraction and metaphysics: Quartz crystals and magnets combined along with copper make a threefold energy resulting in extremely powerful abilities to manifest intentions, raise vibrational frequencies, and healing abilities. The thought is carried along the magnetic emanations to all animate and inanimate objects to influence and direct through the power of the will. Therefore the force of the will is amplified and intensified while holding the wand. To bring magnetism into your body, in addition to drinking magnetized water, hold the wand in the left hand and imagine the magnetic energy flowing through the wand into your body. To amplify and intensify your intention hold the wand in the right hand and bring your consciousness to the third eye. Then move your consciousness to the back of the head and imagine the thing desired being placed in your hand. Say "I will this become actual in my life." Then take some *action* toward realizing that goal. Feel the joy in receiving whatever it is you are imaging as being given to you. By your intentions and the Law of Attraction whatever you are imaging will connect through the magnetic field and attract it to you.

I rent booths at psychic fairs and metaphysical shows traveling around the southeast. I don't have much success usually breaking even after expenses were paid. The Mind, Body, and Spirit Expo in Raleigh, North Carolina is profitable. I sell about twenty-six wands. A Cherokee Indian woman comes up to me and we discuss twenty twelve. I'm obsessed with the "end date" of December twenty-first, twenty twelve predicted by the Mayans.

A friend of mine tells me I'm so gullible I will believe anything. He says, "You know gullible is not in the dictionary?"

"Really?"

"Freedom," she says. "It's all about freedom and the end of control. There will be no more prisons. We will be free; cosmic freedom!"

Our meditation group meets at Ginny and Lyndsey's house. We also meditated at my house in the circle that appeared in my yard. Then we meet at Cynthia and Carol's house. Cynthia lives in the house where Susan and I had lived at seventeen fifty Vestaview. She is the one who bought the house when we had to move. One night we visit an abandoned house "up on the hill" where Cynthia believes black magic had been practiced. We take pictures of all kinds of orbs that are floating around the place and get a "sick to the stomach" feeling and photograph a rather nasty looking brown deformed orb. It's unlike most of the colorful, perfectly symmetrical orbs we had photographed in the past. We take several pictures of this brown orb. Every time we take a picture it moves from the previous photograph so we knew it wasn't "dust specks." In my mind's eye the orb follows us back to Cynthia's house and waits outside. The other girls can "see" it too. When I leave, the orb rides with me in the car back to my house. When I get home, the orb follows me in to my wand making room and is instantly dissolved!

I go to Atlanta to have a cranial-sacral massage. A friend of mine, Pat, who lives near there had gone to a place called Centerpoint Therapies and she was so pleased with it that she recommends that I go there. The massage therapist, Sharon Price, administers the massage. (This type of massage is not "hands on," but consists of an energetic light touch that manipulates the membranes and fluid that protects the brain, spinal and nervous system). I lie down on the massage table on my back. She starts at my feet and works her way up to my head. When she reaches the back of my neck my whole brain fills with light. She asks me if there's anything that I feel that I need to get rid of. I tell her I have a lot of guilt (about my addiction and its effects on my children and the women I have selfishly used) accumulated over the years. She begins the massage underneath my stomach and moves toward my chest. When she gets to my head I can feel an "entity" moving up toward my third eye chakra.

"What do you feel?" she asks.

"Guilt," I say unsurely.

"Release it!" she says.

"I can't," I say.

"Why?"

"It doesn't want to go."

"Ask it to leave."

"It doesn't want to go."

She then tells "it" that it's time to go, its time had been served, and she gives it permission to leave my body.

It feels like I was trying to give birth to something through my third eye. (Not painful, but as if there was a balloon coming out of this area). There is swoosh and it's gone! I have not had any guilt since then.

# Chapter Fourteen

## *Magic Spells*

I had previously met Eric's friends, Nancy and Elizabeth, both of whom are practicing Wiccans. I make them all wands and they love them! We decide to do a powerful spell together. Elizabeth is an excellent spell writer. We meet one night and cast the spell in a closed pentagram shaped circle. I'm not scared, as these girls know what they're doing. Elizabeth writes the spell and while standing in the circle we repeat the words in unison while facing the four directions. (North, South, East, West) For the next three weeks we repeat the spell in unison at nine a.m. every morning in our separate homes. The spell reads: Spirit: May our spirits continue to be filled with peace, love, prosperity, and the good will to all as our blessings with love, health, and wealth continue to lead us on our journey throughout the year with knowledge, wisdom, and understanding. Earth: Mother Earth, we thank you for continuing to bless us with strength to heal what we can. Ground us with the ability to do so. May we continue to be filled with the fruits of the earth. Air: As the universe continues to flow within us, let the healing love flow from us, keeping our spirits light. Let the wind refresh us with thoughts of peace.

Fire: As our power continues to grow within us, let the fire within us burn that, which is negative. Fire, burn within us the desire to do what needs to be done.

Water: The water flows through us daily to cleanse us of that we do not need. As it cleanses the wrong, the right continues to flow outward into that which it is meant to be, the good of all. So mote it be!

With the last words as we hold our wands in the air, a powerful wind begins to blow from the east. It must have worked because I do have a prosperous year. I buy a motorcycle and a new car.

I lose my fear of the unknown. I'd always wanted to channel because I read about it all my life. I have a sponsee, Carl, who has been channeling information from Venus. He receives a message from her that says at nine twenty-one (twenty-one, twenty-one military time or twelve,

twelve backwards) there's a message I need to receive. So that night I quiet my mind to allow the message to come through. This is what it says:

"I am so grateful for you Son, John. Continue on your path. We have much work for you to do. Big changes are coming. We want you to start channeling messages to the world to prepare them for our coming. It is important that you become a channel of our peace. Tell them all is well and that we mean no harm. The world as you know it will fade away and a new earth will take its place. This will be all for now. Adonai."

"We want to prepare the world for our arrival. You will be given instructions on how to do this. We will take you into our ships and teach you. You will become a teacher. This will get easier as you learn to channel us. See, nothing to fear! (They knew I had some fear about channeling). More instructions will be forthcoming. We are honored that you allowed us to come."

Then I asked them who "they" were.

"We are the Council of Seven. We have been guiding you along. We have much to tell you, but this is an introduction."

In another session the message says:

"We wish to communicate now. You have been appointed as the "wand maker." We wish you continue to make wands. You made them before in Atlantis. We have been following your progress." Then I asked them who they were.

"We are the Sons of Light. This is your destiny. We want you to channel our message to the world. We want you to meet with us. The cities will come down from the sky."

I don't know who these beings are or whether it's my subconscious or entities from another realm. I have not channeled since. I continue to make wands and with the help of Hoyt improve the design by placing a spring in the bottom and securing the crystals and magnets with a steel pin. My dreams of success in exhibiting at the metaphysical shows are thwarted. However, I did meet a lot of great people who thought like me and I learned many new ideas. One of these is the nature of chlorine and fluoride in the water supply, both of which are deadly poisons that I'm consuming and soaking in! I buy a Berkey water filter for my drinking water and a "bath ball" for my bath water to filter out the chlorine. (The Environmental Protection Agency released two reviews of research on fluoride. One of the studies found that prolonged, high intake of fluoride can increase the risk of brittle bones, fractures and crippling bone abnormalities. *The Associated Press* Published Friday, January seven, twenty eleven, eight forty-five PM EST)

I begin hypnosis sessions with Eric. He's adamant about raising his psychic energy so he can write a book about his abilities. We meet once a week and I hypnotize him. We write a script to raise his energy. I use a crystal necklace to invoke the trance state. This is good not only for raising your energy but also to meditate with. I use the visualizations at our group meditations.

Keep your eyes focused on the crystal. Listening to the sound of my voice I want you to concentrate on the crystal. Your eyes get heavier with each passing of the crystal. In a few moments, I'm going to count down from nine. When I reach the number one you will close your eyes and become completely relaxed. Nine . . . eight . . . seven . . . six . . . five . . . four . . . three . . . two . . . one, *close your eyes.* You are completely relaxed. You are concentrating on my voice and nothing else. I want you to see yourself in a meadow. You feel the grass beneath your feet and the sun on your skin. You take deep breaths, enjoying the fresh air and becoming more relaxed with each breath. You are concentrating on my voice listening to every command I give you. You see a forest about thirty feet away. As you walk towards the forest, you become more relaxed with each step. You reach the forest and you are completely relaxed. You notice light that filters through the trees. You walk towards the light and you are completely relaxed and will listen and retain every command I give you. Your old programming is just that, "old programming!" You have complete trust in me and in yourself. You release all of your past doubts and fears.

(Repeat three times) You reach the light and step into a river. You step into the river and reach out your hands to absorb all the energy of the river. You feel the energy of the river coursing through you. As the energy from the river enters your body, you are cleansed of your doubts, fears, and blocks. (Repeat three times)

You relinquish control of yourself as the water's cleansing energy flows through you. The control you need consciously is not needed in this refuge. This is your Heaven. You are peace. Your bodily fears, doubts, and blocks are gone. You are now completely cleansed and are a clean slate. The water has washed away all negativity. (Repeat three times) To your right you notice a cave. You step out of the river. You walk towards the cave retaining the energy you absorbed from the river. The cave is dark and deep. You walk deeper into the cave. You reach a cove of crystals. Every color surrounds you. You absorb the energy. You touch a clear quartz crystal. As you place your hand on the crystal you are instilled with a sense of accomplishment. Anything you set your mind to accomplish, you can. You cannot shake the energy you receive. You see a purple crystal and place your right hand on it. As you touch the purple crystal you are filled with a sense of self-love. You cannot shake the energy you receive from the purple crystal. Next you place your hand on a blue crystal. The blue crystal fills your body with a sense of wisdom, knowledge, and understanding. Everything you have worked on in your lifetimes enters your brain and being. You cannot shake the energy you receive from the crystal. Next, you see a golden yellow crystal. You place your hand on the crystal and are filled with a sense of confidence and success. You are confident and certain with your success. You cannot shake the energy you receive from the crystal. The last crystal you place your hand on is a bright green. Prosperity fills you completely. Money is drawn to you. You cannot shake the energy you receive from the green crystal. You now see a magnetic block. You place your left hand on the block and absorb the magnetic energy of the block. You are now able to see and connect with the magnetic field of all animate and inanimate objects. You are able to connect to this magnetic field and manipulate it. (Repeat three times)

Your will is now able to direct its thoughts along the path of this magnetic field to fulfill its commands. Imagine you have reached the goal you are trying to accomplish. You are now using your winnings (he wanted to bet on dogs) to write your book. You are now using the money to publish your book. You are now paying someone to write your book. See yourself taking the manuscript to a publisher. See the book in its published form. You are now using the money to travel and promote your book. (Repeat three times)

Funny, as I am editing this, I realize I was hypnotizing myself! The book is *my book*.

All of the energy you receive from the crystals and from the river is at your manipulation. When you are conscious you will be able to manipulate these energies when you hear this phrase, "As above, so below." (Repeat three times) Now *float* for a little while.

In a few moments now, I'm going to count forwards from one to nine. When I reach the number nine you will awaken, completely refreshed. You will have retained all memory of this session. You will give me feedback on your session tonight. (Repeat three times) One . . . two . . . three . . . four . . . five . . . six . . . seven . . . eight . . . nine, *awaken*.

One session I raise the energy so much in the room it feels like electricity is surging through our bodies. I finally realize that Eric is relying on an outside source to provide him with what he needs. I tell him this and that the source of his power is within him, not me. We abandon our hypnosis sessions.

# Chapter Fifteen

## *Mother*

*"We are continually manipulating God (the universe) for an outcome that we think we should be having instead of being able to receive what is readily given us."*-Michael Brown-"The Presence Portal"

Mother worships the ground my brother and I walk o
in since we have sobered up and neither of us can do no wrong. (My brother gets sober three years after I do). She had fallen at the church several years ago and hit her head. She appears to have recovered from that. When she and my father return from an Alaskan cruise she gets to where she can't walk anymore. We take her to St. Vincent's hospital where they diagnose a

fractured spine. They send her to Lakeshore Rehab; however, her mind stays at St. Vincent's. The summer of two thousand nine consists of hospitals and nursing homes. Her only words are "Bob." "Bob." (My father)

My Father, brother, and I are trying to keep her alive by forcing her to eat and drink. We spoon-feed and make her drink water. She fights every attempt. "Do not resuscitate, do not tube feed, do not keep her alive artificially," are the final instructions we give her doctor. We surrender. Four days later as I sit beside her bed, she's having difficulties breathing. I sense a "crowd" in the room. I go to get the nurse.

"She's drowning," the nurse says.

"You need to call an ambulance." I said.

"You know it's going be like this. They'll take her to the hospital and re-hydrate her and bring her back here to the nursing home and get de-hydrated again." She's right. This is how it had been all summer long.

I try to call Dad. It's late, no answer.

I try to call my brother, no answer.

I tell them to call an ambulance; I just can't bear to stand there and watch her choke to death.

Alone in her room, I cry out to God, "What do you want me to do?"

Nothing is the answer I received.

The ambulance arrives and I send them back.

I wake to the sound of the phone ringing.

"Where are you?" Father asks.

She passed about three hours after I had left. I break down and go to console and to be consoled. My brother and I go to a meeting. I'm numb.

"She wants you to read this at her funeral," Father says. "It's a card you gave her for her birthday some time ago."

"Fuck. You mean I have to read this?" I say, honored and angered at the same time. The note's dated August twentieth, nineteen ninety-eight and says, "Please look inside and read at my funeral. I write too fast but love you-all so much!"

The card reads: "A loving birthday message for my mother. How can I tell you how much your love has meant? How grateful I am for the time we've spent. How can I give back to you in return such steadfast support and unfailing concern . . . how can I thank you for all that you've done, for giving me skills to fight battles I've won, for being my guide, for teaching me how to take the failures in stride. Though words seem inadequate, I'm hoping you see how deeply your caring has influenced me. My dreams and so many points of view were inspired by having a mother like you." Happy birthday, Love, John. (I always have a knack for picking good cards).

She didn't ask me to read it; she only wanted it read at her funeral. I read this to the gathered crowd crying in unison with all who are there. Some idiot relative was taking pictures, really?

Father's admitted to the hospital with bleeding ulcers. He's lost his mate of fifty-five years and has been drinking a lot. When he's released he can't take care of himself without help from my brother, Johnny, and me. We take turns staying with him. Fourteen thousand dollars of my mother's jewelry turns up missing.

Sometime after my mother's death I go see Abraham Hicks in Atlanta. Esther Hicks is a channel for a group of beings that call themselves "Abraham." As I check in to the hotel, Jerry Hicks, Esther's husband, and she are checking in right behind me. During the seminar as Abraham speaks I have the realization that my "higher Self" is not "up there" but envelopes, surrounds and permeates my entire being.

I buy Abraham's book *Money and the Law of Attraction* and imagine money coming in, living in luxurious homes, clients walking in my office causing the little bell hung on the door to ring. I imagine hearing the phone in my office ring and clients giving me money, counting it out on my desk. I begin to live all the practices the book talks about to attract wealth and abundance. I combine that with *A Course in Miracles*. I program an abundance mentality rather than lack and poverty. I realize that I'm the source of my abundance by the thoughts I think. I get results. I believe it'll work. I reprogram my mind. Am I worthy of abundance? My parents had always complained about money. "We don't have it." "We can't afford it," had been programmed into my mind from an early age. So naturally when my boys ask me for money, the response is, "I don't have it. I can't afford it." I keep perpetuating lack. This is an illusion. I finally realize abundance or not, no matter what I think, what I do, nothing can happen to me that my Higher Self (God) does not will for me. I cannot change the wind. (Or can I?)

I hate my job. I'm sick of fighting and arguing all the time. I go to the Mind, Body, and Spirit expo in Raleigh in February twenty ten to sell my wands. I had some success there in September after mother died. I love Raleigh. There is a lot of spiritual energy there along with people who support it. A woman comes up to me thirty minutes before the Raleigh show is over and we start talking about my job and how I hate it.

She says, "What is your talent? Tune in to that. What is your passion? It may be something you have done in the past. What do you do that comes easy for you and that you can't believe other people have such a hard time doing it?"

She tells me I must change my belief in the court system because my current belief says that it is broken and there's no justice. So I keep attracting people who are broken and there's no justice. When I discover what my heart tells me to do she says this is where my fortune lies. The revelation that the only reason for coming here is to receive this message hits me hard. On the way home the nine-hour drive gives me time to contemplate. What have I done all my life? Service and dealing with people. I love people. What can I do in service to help a person that comes easy to me? What is my passion? Align my work with something that has to do with my belief in people and the goodness in them. Align that with the belief in the goodness of the universe. How can I "save the world" or contribute to that. How does it benefit others, the universe and me? I love to inspire people and make them feel better about themselves. I love to make people laugh. Is it crafting? (Wand making). Keep asking questions. What is it that brings *joy*?

I don't have to figure it out. It will just come in when I start to let go of the old job. Quit resisting. Quit trying to figure it out, it's unfigureoutable, just *let go*. The old will fade away and the new will come in. It will be gradual. Let the old job go and the new one will show up. I can't save the world; I can only navigate through the court system to the best of my abilities. I can't control outcomes. I need to give and support rather than having the illusion of controlling outcomes. My ego wants me to acquire things, money, women, jobs, and houses in order to be happy. When I get these material things, the ego says I want more. The ego knows not what it wants. There are no bad things that happen, only good. (God) I return home with hope.

I have a criminal case in Opelika. My client has been caught with a "mini meth lab" in his shoulder bag while he visited the dealer. The police had tricked them into letting them in the house by asking for a glass of tea. I'd prepared the night before to get the case thrown out based on an illegal search. I meet with the prosecutor and she offers my client fifteen years, split three years, which means that he'll spend three years in prison and be on probation for fifteen. I take the offer to my client and he refuses. We break for lunch. I counter offer ten years and probation. The prosecutor counters with fifteen years and she won't oppose applying for probation. I tell my client to take it and the judge will probably grant probation although I have no idea what this judge will do since it's my first time in Opelika court. We decide to take our chances. I fill out the paperwork and I'm waiting on the judge to call us up for the plea.

"The judge says, "Who's next?"

Another lawyer and I stand up at the same time. I tell the other lawyer to go ahead in front of me. While the other lawyer is standing before the judge the prosecutor gets up and goes to talk to the detectives. She comes back to me and offers fifteen years, split thirty days. My client had already spent thirty days in jail.

We take the plea and as we're leaving the courtroom, my client turns to me and says, "You know this would have never happened if you had not let that other lawyer go first!" I realize that God's working the courtroom, not me!

I still hate my job and Dave instructs me to just sit in it for now and be open to messages from God. Follow the "signs" and let it go he tells me.

He says, "Don't try and control your spiritual path. Value what you do; you are good at it!"

# Chapter Sixteen

## *Change is Good (God)*

*"Change is an announcement that something is not working."*- Neale Donald Walsh

I get restless, irritable, and discontent, again! Shit. My business has fallen off drastically. I'm struggling to pay my bills. I call my sponsor Dave. I seem to work better with him. He knows me. He lives the program.

"Write down three things on what John thinks the problem is," he instructs. Share this at meetings, "I don't want to share, but it's suggested that I do because my ego and false pride doesn't want me to."

I want to paint a picture that everything is okay, but I'm full of fear and I hate my job! I'm tired of fighting and arguing all the time. I got into the business because of the money and I thought I could save the world. "Why don't you quit?" people ask me. I can't. There are bills to pay. A lot of people hate attorneys. I hardly ever get any compliments on a job well done. In court you're guilty until proven innocent. The judges play God, most of the cops lie and the system is all fucked up as it's all about the money and control. Who are you going to believe, a uniformed "officer" or a crack addict/dope dealer? What's *really* going on with John?

Get into the solution. Work step one, again. I'm powerless and my life is unmanageable because I am trying to manage it! False pride becomes the reverse side of fear. I'm trying to cover up my deep lying inferiorities-the persistent sense of inadequacy *or* the tendency to diminish myself. I'm trying to run on self-sufficiency and not trusting and relying on God to provide me what I need. I'm creating my own drama and just making up bullshit. I'm consumed by how work should be rather than the way it is; no justice, no laws except what the particular judge says it is in whatever courtroom I'm in. If only I can get the job the way *I think* it should be and get my bills paid, *then* I'd be happy.

Dave tells me this is the disease (dis-ease) of alcoholism. It creates the illusion that if my job goes like I think it should be and my bills are paid I'll be okay. I'm trying to control the outcome of my spiritual growth and finances. My spiritual practices, praying, and meditating are not working anymore and no relief from me can be found. I'm looking for a material solution to a spiritual problem. The problem is John. He (the ego) got in the way of the connection between God and me. I blame outside "things" for the way I feel. It's an inside job.

"You need to try different routines," Dave says.

"Play the drums."

"Ride your motorcycle."

"Pray at night instead of the morning."

I'm trying to control the outcome of my spiritual growth rather than allowing God to lead me. The disease of alcoholism is just making up bullshit. The topic of discussion I lead one night is bullshit. People are still talking about that one; it's a great meeting!

Quality of activity is the key, not quantity. The quantities of spiritual growth cease working because I'm trying to control and direct them. I follow his instructions. Riding my motorcycle and playing the drums is my meditation. I had to quit thinking so much, that's the problem. I have to let God direct my spiritual growth. He knows what is best. I have to be open to His messages. My old solutions do not apply to today's problems. They must be given, not controlled as I had been trying to do. I have to be careful about the "signs" from God. "Quite often, however, the thoughts that seem to come from God are not answers at all. They prove to be well-intentioned unconscious rationalization . . . he may have forgotten the possibility that his own wishful thinking and the human tendency to rationalize has distorted his so called guidance." *Twelve Steps and Twelve Traditions*

"It's just a job, it's not who you really are. It's just a game. The ego has made up this clutter and you need to un-clutter your mind in order to be led to the solution," Dave tells me.

He says, "This is why most people don't make it in AA. They do all this work and it quits working and they say the short version of the serenity prayer. Fuck it. And they go back out and drink." My first sponsor goes back out and drinks at nineteen years sober!

I follow his instructions and play the drums in the afternoon and ride my motorcycle. I pray the St. Francis Prayer on my knees at night. I get away from myself. I get relief from me by not thinking! One afternoon I'm riding my motorcycle and the thought of how great it is to be out on the open road, no cares or worries, and feeling the wind in my face and I thank God for letting me ride today. I immediately look to my right and see a church sign that says, "Thank you God for giving me peace beyond human understanding."

I'd been putting an honest effort into my spiritual growth but the motives underlying the actions are to control the outcome to make me feel better. I'm trying to understand and control something that is neither understandable nor controllable. I'm trying to manufacture the peace, the joy and the love that only God gives. I'm trying to control and manipulate my spiritual growth to achieve the outcome I think is best for me! The words cunning, baffling, and powerful take on a new meaning.

I abandon my expectations. I surrender self (ego) and outcomes. What I think I can expect docs not work. I substitute my negative thoughts of imagined problems with new thoughts. I meet with Dave again and I write down the three new thoughts as he instructs me. When I think a negative thought about my job or my finances he tells me to substitute these words instead:
This thought is *a part* of my alcoholism. I am removing/abandoning this thought.

"What did you write?" he asks.

"A part of my alcoholism."

"This thought *is* my alcoholism," he says. "See?"

"Holy shit," I say realizing how the subconscious disease of alcoholism plays on me.

"I don't know what God's will is for me, but I *will* abandon myself to it," I write.

"Wait a minute. What did you write?" he asks.

"I *will* abandon myself to it."

"That's not what I said. I *am* abandoning myself to it," he tells me.

"Fuck!" I say, realizing just how cunning, baffling, and powerful the disease (or ego) is. My disease writes down an act in the future, not now!

"Do the next thing in front of you," he says.

I put into action what he tells me. At night I review my thoughts that happened during the day, putting them on paper in black and white. This helps me see what the nature of the problem is. The nature of the problem is me! I don't know what the solution is. The solution is outside of me. I can't understand the disease of alcoholism! I notice that my thoughts are nothing more than thoughts. I'm only attacking myself, again, shit. I go on a golf outing to Myrtle Beach. I'm miserable because I take myself and attack thoughts with me. I let "worldly clamors" dominate my thinking. The disease of alcoholism is relentless and I must be just as tenacious and relentless as *it* is or I will drink again. My desires for security and material comfort oppose the Grace of God. I want my circumstances (bills paid, job) changed, *then* I'll be happy. I realize that my life circumstances are the illusion and God, not me, is the solution. I get more relief from me, which *is* the problem.

Father is doing a lot better and he calls one day while I'm at work and says, I want to take you and Billy on a twelve day Mediterranean cruise. Can you go?

"Are you fucking me?" I say while clearing my calendar. "Hell yeah!"

I thought the date of August twenty-fourth, two thousand ten would never arrive. The day before we leave I'm demanding God provide answers to my life situation. A song comes on the radio that I like. I look down at the title, *It's Just Not Meant to Be*, by Tame Impala at the same time a "loud" voice in my head says, "Your service is needed elsewhere."

I think, "Okay, I'm done practicing law and mean it."

An immediate and overwhelming sense of relief comes over me and a heavy weight lifts off my shoulders. A whole world of unlimited possibilities opens up to me. I leave on the cruise a free man and have the best time of my life!

We go to Barcelona a day before the ship leaves. I *love* it! My brother and I take off walking the streets; my body is filled with wonder and awe as I am fully conscious and alive. I take in the energy through every pore of my body and allow myself to be guided. My brother comments on his disbelief that we never get lost. I tell him that I let go of trying to figure it out. I booked my tours to go alone as this gives me a chance to explore without interference from brother's ego. The people on the ship in their walkers, wheelchairs, and wrinkles dash all hopes of getting laid. Everyone is asleep by nine.

We stop at Nice, Cannes, Florence, Pisa, Dubrovnik, Split (I comment, "There ain't shit in Split."), Venice, Sorrento, and Pompeii. As the tour guide talks and gives a history of Pompeii, I lean against the wall. A piece of the wall breaks off in my hand.

I think, *Oh shit*. Then look around and place the rock in my pocket.

Cruises are a good way to see a lot of places in a short period of time and to determine where I might go for a longer period. I didn't have to pack and unpack. The stops were too brief, except for Venice which we stayed overnight. I always like to sample the local cuisine, and I have one of the best meals of my life sitting on one of the canals eating a four course meal of lasagna.

I return from vacation and arrive at the house exhausted. I see the back door is boarded up.

*Shit, I've been evicted*, I think.

I walk around to the front door and notice my forty-seven inch flat screen and CD player missing. Finally getting to sleep I awake the next morning and call my friend who's been keeping an eye on the place. He had spent the night, left for work and comes back that afternoon to find the door kicked in. He questions the neighbors who tell him they'd seen a white van leaving the driveway. My youngest son has a white van.

I think, *The little bastard!*

He had taken my motorcycle earlier in the year without permission. He broke the front steering lock and sawed the lock off the back tire. He'd pawned my gun about a month earlier. I'd kicked him out of the house and told him not to call me. My landlord comes over and notices the double-keyed deadbolt lock is unlocked. There are only two people with keys. I'm so fucking mad I can spit nails, those fucking bastards. They'd (being ex-wife and son) known about the trip and apparently broke into my house on the day after I told them I was leaving. The deadbolt was unlocked, which meant that they unlocked the door, stole the TV and then made it look like a break-in. They forgot to lock the dead bolt back.

A month later I receive a pawn ticket in the mail addressed to my ex-wife stating a pawn is about to expire on eleven eleven, two thousand ten. (Repeating numbers, again).

"What the fuck is this," I think while calling the pawnshop to see if it was *my TV*.

"It's a Vizio flat screen," they tell me.

"Not mine."

I contact the sheriff's office and tell the sergeant about the pawn ticket.

"What's the serial number?"

I give it to him and he says, "Here it is at a pawnshop on First Avenue! She pawned that and a CD player on August twenty-seventh, the day of the break in. She and your son have been pawning jewelry, too."

That fucking bitch! That bastard!

"We'll have a warrant for you to sign in the next couple of days. When you sign the warrant, you can get your TV and CD player back."

"Good! She'll sing like a bird when she gets arrested," I say.

My oldest son confesses to the theft of my mother's jewelry. I swear out a warrant for my ex.

# Chapter Seventeen

## *The Farm*

A close friend of mine, Carol, calls me one day and says, "You have to turn on Oprah and see "John of God."

I watch the show and it is about a man in Brazil they call John of God. He is a metaphysical healer who cures cancer, AIDS, paralysis, and surgically removes tumors while in trance states. I am always fascinated by "alternative treatments" and believe there is a cure for everything in nature. I store this show in my memory.

I decide to go into partnership with a man who owns some land down in Sawyerville. Carol had sent him to me several years ago and I drew up an LLC for him. He's all fired up about his vision of a certified organic farm and needed some help in turning his property into an organic farm. I didn't think much about it until I returned from

Europe. I go down to look at the property and the only thing growing is cedar trees. Not a problem as I'm an expert on farming and have spent the last twenty years growing vegetables in my back yard. I'm lit on fire by his enthusiasm and I invest in renting bulldozers, laying two thousand feet of irrigation, building a well, equipment, and think *this* is the wave of the future. I study about farming, NOP, growing, planting, and bought a motor home to live in and a farm tractor to ride on. I do all the certification, marketing, speaking, designing, and investing. We get everything ready on July fourth, twenty eleven, plant, fertilize, and water. Nothing grows. I should have known that cedar trees grow in soil that has *tons* of magnesium. In other words, the soil might as well be sterile. I can figure this out. We plant yellow crookneck squash and it starts to grow. We plant okra and it starts to grow. My partner never shows up until the day we go to market. I'm running a three acre farm, alone. It's a thousand miles from nowhere and if I could have built a farm in a worse place . . .

The squash starts to have green splotches and looks like those Thanksgiving table decorations with knots all over them. There's a fucking fungus in the soil that gets in all the cucurbit vegetable family and the stores won't buy funny looking knotty vegetables.

It's September, twenty eleven and we go to Rome for a twelve day cruise with stops in Athens, Santorini, Istanbul, Ephesus, Mykonos, and the Isle of Capri. This time the ship is void of canes, walkers, wheel chairs, and wrinkles. The first night I go with Father to the main dining room where I am placed with people from all over the world. Anastasia and Gurli from Denmark sit down at our table. We instantly form a friendship. Ana is ten years older, very wise, and open-minded; Gurli is one month older than me, attractive, blonde haired, and blue eyed. I catch her looking at me all during dinner. The three of us form a manwhich (I'm in the middle of them, clothes on) in the hammock and talk and laugh non-stop late into the night.

I go to Mykonos with my brother and then to the island of Delos where the God Apollo was born and the Oracle of Delphi. The legends say that more light falls on this island than anywhere in the world except Hawaii. Scientists have actually measured and confirmed this.

I'm wearing my usual light t-shirt and baggie carpenter pants, camera on my belt, lathered up with sun block. Delos dates to the eighth century, BC. We follow the tour guide and eventually wander off on our own. Billy is red as a beet.

I turn to him and say, "Damn Billy, I sure would like to get a piece of Delos."

"Why don't you get a piece of marble?" he says as he looks around.

"Okay."

"Here's one," he says while he lifts up a legal pad size stone.

"Shit, Billy," I say while looking around and shoving the stone in my side pocket.

We continue to walk around; the ancient relic reminds me of its presence by continually banging against my thigh. I constantly check to make sure the buttons are secure and nothing is peeking out. I make it back to the ship and empty my pockets to enter the metal detector thinking, *its stone*, while walking cautiously through when the alarm almost breaks the stone in pieces.

Security says, "Sir you have to empty everything out of your pockets."

I look down avoiding eye contact while I reach in my pockets, step around to the other side and find a penny in my right pocket, toss it in the bucket and step through the silence.

That night the girls and I decide to go out. I'm on top of the world. We call a cab and decide to go to a square where most of the tourists are going. Belly dancing, local flavor, and good times are the forecast.

We flag the cab and tell him where we want to go and he says no, "I take you somewhere else, Kum Kopi fish market."

Stepping out of the cab we enter a long alley leading up the hill. The hosts of dozens of restaurants flood us with happy faces speaking a language I cannot comprehend, enticing us to try their delicacies. We burst out of the ally into a large courtyard of tables surrounding a fountain. People are eating, laughing, and music fills the air. The aroma of seafood, hookah's, and love filters through the multi-colored lights circling the local hangout. I ask one of the locals where I can find a Cuban cigar and he points through the courtyard to a shop nowhere to be found. We select a restaurant on the second floor overlooking the courtyard. It was one of the best meals ever! A young man comes up to the table with a bag full of Cubans for sale.

We leave Kum Kopi and hail a cab back to the ship. Anastasia gets in the front and Gurli and I get in the back. We make out all the way back to the ship. Anastasia jerks the door open, slams it, and trudges hurriedly in front of us without a word. Gurli and I decide to go to the top deck and continue what we started.

Several hours later we have to go somewhere. Anastasia is in Gurli's room. Billy and dad are in my room. I know where we can go: the AA room. With the backdrop of Istanbul we have sex behind the locked doors. It becomes a nightly ritual. I have meetings during the day and "meetings" at night. Alcoholics Anonymous is good to me. We part when the cruise ends with hopes that we will be together someday.

I'm going to check on the sterile farm with my pseudo partner, my vision blurs, I can't swallow and my right arm loses all function. I pick it up with my left hand and place it on the window seal. My partner is driving. I'm determined to make the farm grow. I get to the farm and tell pseudo I need to go back and go to the emergency room. I'm diagnosed with a TIA, or fucking stroke as I call it. The Basilar artery in my brain was 70-90% clogged. Surgery was not an option. Blood thinners were.

I get back to my house and the power is cut off for non-payment. I move in with Dad. Great. He plans a trip to Norway. This time he's going by himself. I get a check from a case I had referred to a large law firm and decide to go with him. It takes me four months to accept the fact that I am living with my daddy. I'm fifty-four.

I fly to London a few days before and take a train to South Hampton to meet Dad and cruise to Norway. It's May and cold as shit. I joke with the floating nursing home crew that I must be on the wrong ship as I thought I was going to Miami, not the North Pole. I bought clothes in South Hampton while Dad had nothing but a light jacket. He's eighty-nine.

We return from the trip at twelve midnight and dad falls in the garage. No damage, just tired and weak. He's been on a walker and catheter for a year. The next morning he has a fever of one hundred and four; he's caught pneumonia and the flu. As mother would say, "He's caught his death a cold."

I planted a crop before the trip and was anxious to see how it grew. I work with a friend cutting trees for gas and cigarettes. I can't afford the fee for my law license. My brother and I take turns helping Dad for the next three months. It's too much and we have to hire help.

"You might as well take me on to Elmwood cemetery."

"I can't live like this anymore."

"You need to get a job," he tells me constantly.

I try and control the doctors, the nurses, the orderlies, and the saints. He writes his obituary. I rewrite his obituary, "William R. Long transitioned to the next Great Adventure on August twelfth, twenty twelve."

I see the neighbors and they tell me how he always talked about how proud he was of me. I realize this Creator of Worlds, this Intelligence wanted me to spend some time with him before he passed.

# Chapter Eighteen

## *John of God*

I watch a video interview about how Wayne Dyer is healed from leukemia by John of God. I contact an acquaintance to arrange a trip to Brazil. I research the protocols of "Friends of The Casa De Dom Inacio." There is no fee for treatment; however, I have to pay for an interpreter and room for fifty dollars per day which includes food. I arrive in Abadiania, Brazil and check into Sao Miguel Pousada which is a short walking distance to the Casa. I inquire as to where I can find Tania, my guide.

We take a tour of the Casa as Tania orients me to the protocols and shows me the crystal healing rooms, the store, and the waterfall. She tells me that I have to get permission from the entities (the entities are spiritual beings who are there to help and assist the people and John of God) to visit the waterfall, but they have already told her I can go. There are thousands of people that come every day from all over the world. Buses, cabs, and vans loaded with people constantly fill the dirt roads with dust. Everyone wears white, in a state of prayer and meditation at all times. I enter the Casa area and feel like I have stepped into *The Celestine Prophecy*. The beautiful meditation rock and flower gardens, mango, and papaya trees, flowering hibiscus, butterflies, and hummingbirds are floating all around. The air is crisp and clear. The atmosphere is calming, the wind is brushing against my face, and the energy is electric. I'm in the healing Garden of Eden.

I decide to go down to the waterfall. I stand in line for an hour as there are many people waiting to get under it and they only allow a few people at a time to enter. Everyone is patient and friendly. Wild parrots and birds are flying and singing while the sound of water rushes through the trees.

I carefully make my way up the moss covered rocks and stick my head underneath the falling, energized water. I gasp for breath as the cold powerful water rushes over me. I can only stay under it for a few seconds. The next day I go back and am able to stay completely submerged for several minutes feeling and imagining the water rinsing my body clean inside and out. I suspect the water must flow through a crystal cavern.

The "current room" is where John of God and the entities do the healing. There are crystals four feet high and about two feet in diameter everywhere. There are pews where everyone sits in prayer and meditation creating a "current" of healing energy I can feel. I have to get there early to get a seat. I stay for five hours in prayer and meditation.

Tania is one of the Casa guides and is close to John of God. He wants to see me. I see him three days after I arrive and he schedules me for surgery on Thursday at two o'clock. I go to the current room from seven-thirty to ten. Tania is there to assist me and takes me to the operating room. There are about thirty to forty other people in the room, all requiring surgery of various kinds. I had to specifically tell them what I needed when I got there. (I wanted my clogged artery cleared). Prayers are said for a short period and John of God comes into the room, prays, and performs surgery on all of us at the same time. The spirits work through John of God and you can read pamphlets on who they are. They tell us not to open our eyes during the surgery as I assume there are entities flying all around doing the metaphysical work. The work is the energetic healing on another dimensional level. I felt nothing and repeated prayers for forty-five minutes. We all get a prescription of herbs, crystal light therapy, and are instructed to go back to the room and rest for twenty-four hours.

I get back to the room and lie down. I'm hungry, so I walk down to the cafeteria, and everyone is saying,

"You're not supposed to be here."

"We would have brought you some food."

"You are vulnerable. You need to go back to your room."

"I'm okay and I feel fine," I say to the other guest staying at the Pousada.

I fix my tray of food and take it to the table thinking, *This is a crock of shit.*

As the thought subsides I realize how weak I am and say, "I need to go back to the room."

I make it back to the room before passing out and I finish eating. I won't be leaving the room for twenty-four hours. I go to sleep and immediately fall into a dream. I am outside my body looking in. I see my artery wrapped in a white honeycomb cloth-like substance. I take the herbs as prescribed and don't leave the room until the sentence is up.

I spend the remaining time praying and meditating in the gardens at the Casa. I go to the bookstore where I meditate there surrounded by hundreds of crystals. I see a large Amethyst where I put my head in the cavern of it. I go to the crystal healing rooms and receive crystal light healing where my chakras are treated and aligned. I visit with people from all over the world listening to their stories of being healed from cancer, tumors, AIDS, and stories of crippled people restored to walk again and on and on. It's magical.

I want to heal my eye, too. A small scar still remains from the parasite so I arrange to have an operation on my eye the second week. I am told that this time it will be a physical operation. I arrive at the current room and Tania takes me to the front where John of God is sitting on a "king's chair" with large crystals surrounding him. There is a lone chair in the center where I'm taken and seated. I'm scared shitless. Tania hands him a metal tray and he proceeds to pray as he steps behind me. He removes a butter knife from the tray and holds my left eye open and starts to scrape my eye. I try to remain as still as a metal rod. My foot wiggles uncontrollably. Time slows down and with each scrape of the knife across my eye the surreal ripples of waves move in slow motion back and forth. He throws the knife back on the tray with a metal "clang" and I collapse, totally limp. They wheel me into the recovery room where I am attended to and they place an eye patch over my eye. They film the procedure. I stay in the room for twenty-four hours.

The rest of the journey is spent at the Casa resting and meditating, and I get a ride back to Brasilia with three people I had met who were taking the same flight. I'm told that the entities will continue to work with me for several months when I get back home. No lifting or strenuous exercise for seven days. No sex of *any* kind for forty days! Shit, I almost make it. (Thirty-eight).

I have a follow up appointment at the stroke clinic for March of twenty thirteen. I tell the doctor I have been to see John of God and he healed the artery. They do an MRI. It's gone.

# Chapter Nineteen

## *The Russian*

*"Risking to offer love before receiving it will free me from the continual search for love in the faces of others. "*-Karen Casey

I think it's a good idea to get on Match.com. I create a profile and start sending letters to women. I get no responses except for a woman in Atlanta who responded to a smart ass comment I wrote her. I get an "I'm interested" response from a cute girl who says she lives in the United States, but later confesses to living in Russia. I play along with her game writing back and forth daily. I research "Russian Brides" and become an expert in spotting the scammers. Most of them fall in love with me after a few letters and want me to send them money so they can be with me.

I join Russian dating sites. I read reviews of the legitimate and illegitimate sites. I place a profile on Elena's Models and start communicating with many women. I meet Iryna Mikhalova and she introduces me to her interpreter, Laura. I arrange a trip to Kiev and go meet her. I meet them at the airport and go to Laura's apartment and meet Laura's husband and two daughters who help in the translating. I have a sick feeling in my stomach, but I look at the five foot, four inch tall, blonde hair, blue-eyed Russian model, and forget all about it. We stay in a flat all arranged by the interpreter. Iryna is from Kherson and seems like a genuine, old fashioned woman. She cooks me dinner and feeds me. We go shopping, mostly for her, but I do find a nice Italian leather jacket for three hundred dollars. We have the most passionate sex I ever experienced. She gets a call from her mother saying her dad has fallen ill. I get back home and we Skype and write each other every day.

I show pictures to my sponsor and he says, "She's a professional." My friends say she's scamming me. I say she can't be. She has a daughter. She's so sweet and innocent. I call her my Angel. We send romantic songs to each other and I write poems and letters. She tells me she loves me. I start sending her money. I'm introduced to Mike in Chicago who will do the Visa paperwork for three hundred dollars. He met his wife through Laura in nineteen ninety-five. She is from Kherson and her name is Iryna also. I start to take Russian lessons and she tells me she is starting English classes.

I fly back to Ukraine and I meet her daughter and her best friend. I see where she lives and it's terrible. It's third world. I propose to her on June fourteen, twenty thirteen. (My birthday). I submit the Visa paperwork, but am concerned about some lies I catch her in. Her profile is still active. Her Skype contacts are increasing. Her father dies and she goes to visit her mom for a week at a time. Once, when I try and call her she doesn't answer. When I call from a different number she hangs up when she hears my voice. I hear the tinkling of glasses in the background. She says she needs five thousand, five hundred dollars to straighten out land she had purchased fifteen years earlier. She constantly needs something and I send money. I refuse to send the money and she hangs up on me. It shatters me. I plan a trip to straighten out certain facts that have kept me in torment and to personally deliver the money. I'm constantly checking her emails and analyzing them. I'm tracing the email IP address.

I bring the money with me and visit her in September. I carry ten thousand dollars in a money belt through the airport in Odessa and they stop me in customs. They ask how much money I have and I can't lie so I show them the money belt and they start counting it out on the table. I'm scared shitless thinking they will confiscate it. They don't and I am greeted by Iryna and her "ride." It's a four hour ride to Kherson and I think they're talking about me in Russian the whole time. I hire an interpreter and believe her story. She has documents and we spend three weeks going to the various government offices to "straighten out the paperwork." I meet her mother and she shows me the land. One night while she is in the shower I check her phone and see a message, "Did you get the Visa paperwork I sent you? I love you." Her response, "I love you, kisses." She comes out of the shower and catches me.

"It's from a friend. I was seeing if you trust me."

The next day I hire an interpreter and she tells me the message is from Laura. I'm ready to walk away but want to believe her. I have a lot invested financially, emotionally, and the Visa interview is approaching fast. I'm there another week and she rushes me off to the airport. The plans of importation are kept. I meet Anthony from Washington and we fly back together, stopping off in Vienna. He has met someone in Odessa and we reminisce about our journey. A friend of my brothers is doing the same thing, except he's not getting laid.

I arrive back home and am relieved somewhat but still tormented by the facts. I check her profile and it's still active. I see that she's been online within the last 24 hours. I've been waiting on this, so I set up a fake profile and tell her I'm interested. She takes it hook, line and sinker. I'm left with a twenty-five thousand dollar leather jacket.

# Chapter 20

## *Metanoia*

"As I let go of _____ I am let go from_____." Dave tells me three weeks after the breakup.

I create a Facebook page and friend all her friends telling them she is a professional scam artist working for her pimp, Laura Zhiglio. I report her to all the scam sites, the police, the prosecutor, the FBI, the CIA, the IRS and every institution that exists in the Ukraine and the world. I start to pray. I start to forgive her and myself.

I go back to Centerpoint massage for a session. She tells me she has been communicating with my Higher Self, Ezekiel or Zeke she calls him.

She puts me on the table and I immediately leave my body and start flying through space. I begin to awaken after an hour. I slowly come to and I ask what happened. She tells me she had to take me out of my body in order to "work" on me. My connection between my heart and brain had become "clogged" metaphysically. She had to clear the "passage." I did recall seeing a "tube" connecting the heart and mind and while I was "out" it lit up like a flashlight. She says the mind is used for logic, planning trips, etc. and I had confused the heart and mind. Follow your heart, John.

I ask for change. I live in a make believe world. I make myself believe anything. My mind is a tape recorder that absorbs all that I see and hear. It's the most sophisticated supercomputer in the universe. I am the programmer. Anger, fear, resentment are all self-imposed narcissistic illusions. I want to feel better. I begin to surrender, again. I realize that I was trying to save her (Savior?) and that it is me who is always trying to be saved from my ego.

So this is how it is. I am two beings, one is created by the world (ego) and the other is my eternal being (a God). I may veer off the path of my spirit, get caught up in worldly clamors, see the light, surrender, and awaken stronger, more determined. Everything in my life, the people, the places, the things all happen in perfect order, at the perfect time to show me to my Self. This Creator of Worlds, this Intelligence of the

Universe keeps my heart beating when asleep, keeps me breathing and performs trillions of chemical reactions per second in my body without me thinking about it! Everything I have done, been, seen, felt, experienced, lived within me and without reinforces the belief that I am the master of my own destiny. I am in charge of my own life, not some string puppet drifting along at the whim of something or somebody else. I am the power, not the person, place or thing I have allowed to affect me. I am effected and affecting.

The earth is changing; I can feel it. Something deep within my soul is stirring and my logical egoist mind cannot comprehend it. Is it real? What is real? I start to question this change and I'll hear a song on the radio or someone will say what I am thinking. I'll be reading spiritual literature while listening to interviews and the words I am reading and the voice talking will be synchronized. I think that this short microscopic instant in eternity is my entire existence, that I inhabit my physical body for seventy-five years, then die and float around in heaven forever. Streets paved in gold? Is there a man with a white beard sitting on a thrown? I see corporations capitalize on the current shift in consciousness: Coke-"Open Happiness," Sony-"It's in your DNA," McDonalds-"Give some happiness," and "Open Hearts Pets." Audi-"Truth in Engineering." "The truth" can no longer be hidden. Everything is coming to light. Everything is vibrating. When one speaks of the truth, but the voice vibrates non-truthfully, I can feel it.

Instead of listening to what other people say what they think is real, I prefer to find out for myself instead. I question everything and do my own research. I go within and find the Kingdom of God, Heaven, peace, joy, and the love I always searched for. It's not "out there." It's not what other people say it is. If I don't go within, I go without. I have learned that information is knowledge and knowledge is wisdom. If something I read or listen to has a "ring of truth" then I follow it. When someone says, "I'll pray for you," I tell them please don't. That may interfere with my spiritual growth!

I try to love the earth (I've been called a tree hugger) because she supports me. I try to love my fellow human, as they are one with me. (Doesn't mean I have to like them!) I try to remember who I really am. *The Course* says, "I am not my body." "I am spirit." I have a host of angels surrounding and guiding me. I don't need protection, cannot die, and am an eternal spiritual being having a human experience.

Quantum physics, quantum entanglement and torsion fields all show that we are all connected to each other. We effect and are affected by one another and all creation. Literally thousands of books have been written on these subjects.

Physicists describe "dark matter" and "dark energy" as being the stuff that makes up ninety-four to-ninety-six percent of our universe. Only four percent is visible matter. It is our thoughts and feelings that create the matter from this energy. We really do create our own reality. (*The Field*, by Lynne Mctaggart, *The Divine Matrix*, by Gregg Braden, *Law of Attraction*, Esther and Jerry Hicks). Time is not speeding up, consciousness is. Science is catching up with spirituality. Why do placebos work? (*You are the Placebo*, Dr. Joe Dispenza) I am a Creator, not the Creator. My consciousness does affect matter.

The religions, governments and "rulers" have taken power away as I let them. The rulers are the demons, devils, Archons, Annunaki, all the same, just different names. (See David Icke, Michael Tellinger, Nag Hammadi texts and many others) A house divided cannot stand. I try to follow the Inner Wisdom within me. I try and align my Inner Being (a God) with my outer being (ego).

Today I take my power back instead of being forced into slave-ship by other human beings who have no control over me. I make my Declaration of Independence, my Declaration of Private Sovereignty as a Divine Human Being. I renounce any and all implied contracts I never agreed to and were forced onto me at birth by the corporation of the United States and state of Alabama through the "birth certificate," driver's license, social security registration, etc. This is contrary to the Declaration of Independence and the Constitution of the United States of America. I am under the laws of my Eternal Being and the Universal Intelligence which guides all things. I am not and will not be a slave to rules that were created at the whim of another human being who has no authority to rule over me. As long as I cause no harm to another human being, I am free.

Jesus said, "This heaven will pass away, and the one above it will pass away. The dead are not alive, and the living will not die. In the days when you consumed what is dead, you made it what is alive. When you come to dwell in the light, what will you do? On the day when you were one you became two. But when you become two, what will you do?" -Gospel of Thomas (left out of the Bible for obvious reasons).

All religions and spiritual teachings say the same thing. Love is the answer and we are all Gods.

"We found the Great Reality deep down within us," says Alcoholics Anonymous

"Is it not written in your law, I said, Ye are all Gods?"-St John 10:34

"…If ye have faith, and doubt not, ye shall not only do this…, but also if ye shall say unto this mountain, Be thou removed, and be thou cast into the sea; it shall be done."-St. Matthew 21:21

"And all things, whatsoever ye shall ask in prayer, ye shall receive." St. Matthew 21:22

"You, dear children, are from God and have overcome them, because the one who is in you (a spirit, a God) is greater than the one who is in the world." (ego) John 4:4

# Chapter 21

## *Dreaming the Living*

My brother and I inherit about two hundred thousand dollars each from the estate of my Father and I'm blowing through it like there is no tomorrow. I take a trip to Southern France with William & Clare Henry. It's a Mary Magdalene themed tour where we trace the footsteps of the Cathar's. We stay at the Les Ducs de Joyeuse hotel which is a sixteenth century castle remodeled and it's fabulous. The "Jesus" story is totally different from Western beliefs. (Did you know the letter J was not invented until 1601?). The landscape is magical and mysterious. I expect fairies and dragons to start flying out of the treetops.

We go to Montsegur where the Knights Templar made their final "stand" against the marauding Roman Catholic Church "Crusaders." The group goes one way and I go another as I want to be alone and meditate on the side of the hill. As I'm walking down to find a place to lie in the grass I find a marker with an "X" on it. This marks the spot where I decide to meditate. I lie down and immediately think, *Why don't they leave us alone. We just want to worship our own way.* In my "mind's eye" I see a beam of light come through the ground, pierce my heart and continue into the sky. I have a profound love and sadness all at the same time and began to weep insatiably. I then meet up with the group as we travel down the mountain. I mention what happened to Nancy, one of the guides. We get to the bottom where the Crusader's burned everyone at the stake (because they wouldn't believe like the church wanted them too) and we all say a prayer.

We then meet at a restaurant nearby to eat lunch. After about five minutes, Nancy comes up to me and says, "John, my spirit guides told me what happened to you."

"Tell me," I say, and she says, "When you were here in a previous lifetime, you tried to save your two wives and the Crusaders killed all of you." This hits me hard. I've been trying to "save" women for 700 years! My two wives in *this* lifetime have died! I told a friend about it and he said, "I don't believe in reincarnation." I say, "That's what you said last time."

We go to Carcassonne where the Spanish Inquisition was held. It's foreboding and everyone feels the death and torture that happened here. One of the group members, a retired neurosurgeon, has visions of being tortured and carried off in a wheelbarrow in pieces. We start to walk around the interior of the outer wall and start to panic. We feel smothered and lose our sense of direction. We finally find our way out and are relieved. We go to Rennes Le Chateau where a poor priest, Berenger Sauniere, was assigned to the town. He discovered something there and suddenly became extremely wealthy and remolded the castle to honor Mary Magdalene. The "story" there is that she came to this area after the "crucifixion" and had twins. She taught the original teachings of the Christ some of which can be found in ancient texts that were left out of the Bible when it was put together at The Council of Nicaea in 325 CE.

I put down a deposit for an Egypt tour with William Henry at the same time I booked the France tour. I find a house that had been in foreclosure located on three acres of land in Munford, Alabama for twenty thousand dollars and remodel it. (I was running out of the inheritance!) It is the perfect setting to finish the book. I have to cancel the Egypt trip. I meet a woman in AA and ask her, "How long do you have sober?" She says nine months, so I take her hostage and move her in. She had nine minutes sober . . . You know the ending to that story. I didn't drink or smoke crack, though! She had a real good decorating eye and made the place a home. I had to move her out in March, twenty fifteen. Another self-examination, shit.

In December of twenty sixteen, I hear an interview about a group, Khemitogy, that was taking a tour in the spring and I book it. We stay at the Le Meridian with views of the Pyramids. My lifelong dream trip since Kindergarten! Mainstream archeologists have no clue how the Pyramids were built, although they have come up with some ridiculous theories. There was an advanced civilization that existed pre-flood and pre-cataclysm more spiritual and advanced than current civilization. The group consists of several engineers, a geologist, an Egyptologist, singers, vocalists, researchers and me. I bring levity to the group, "There's fucking Pyramids everywhere," I'd say. "Bless their fucking hearts," I'd quip. At the end of the tour, everyone is saying bless their fucking hearts and I'm so fucking grateful. The vocalist would "tone" in all the temples and inside the Kings Chamber of the Great Pyramid, so beautiful, it resonates to the soul. We meditate inside the Kings Chamber for two hours, taking turns lying in the granite box. When I walk out, I feel cleansed from head to toe, resetting my DNA.

We go to the Cairo Museum and find a granite box tucked away in a corner. Apparently, this advanced civilization, some twelve thousand years ago, were cutting the granite box with a huge double bladed saw. They veered "off line," like you do when you cut wood, and left the box unfinished. You can see the blade marks left in the granite.    We see evidence of large drill holes in granite that are at numerous sites we visit.

We go to Aswan where the Obelisk were quarried and see the "Unfinished Obelisk" where this civilization quarried a twelve hundred ton piece of granite, found a crack in it and left it in the ground.    Mainstream archeologists say they quarried it by chipping it with a black rock; moved it over hills with rope, loaded it in a boat, then lifted it in place on a base that was perfectly equidistant and level.    We don't have the cranes nor equipment to do that today!    You can see where some type of machine came down from the top and scooped the granite out.    Transported it with rope . . . That's funny.    There is not enough leverage to beat the granite with rocks.    Who would volunteer to hit that last lick?

"On March fifth, twenty seventeen, twenty-five individuals representing six countries met for the first time as group at the Le Meridien hotel in Cairo, Egypt. A unique heart energy was created. Fourteen days later, having been transformed by a shared magical experience, they parted ways and returned to their respective parts of the world, dispersing their heart energy across the glove. This group is dedicated to sharing their stories, photos and love of their adventure together. God bless them all."-David Champeau, creator of the Facebook Group Egypt Techno-Spiritual Travelers twenty seventeen.

In March of twenty eighteen, I take a trip to Sedona, Arizona on a Psychic Awareness Retreat with friends I meet on Facebook. I had met Lisa Najjar, author of *Dying to Tell You, Channeled Messages of the Famously Dead* numerous years ago and she and Patricia Monna, Psychic Medium and International Law Enforcement intuitive, put the retreat together. A good friend of mine had moved out there eight years ago and I wanted to see him while I was there.

The Saturday after we arrived, we do a fire ceremony wherein we write a letter to God. We ask for Him to show us a sign that he got our letters. I ask for a rainbow. We place the letters into the fire and send it out into the Universe. At that moment, ten Javelina's had gotten into the retreat area and were standing about twenty feet from the fire. Lisa looks up the metaphysical meaning of ten and pigs. Good fortune, prosperity, and luck!

The next day I contact my friend and he wants to take me to an AA meeting that he is chairing that night. I contact him to come pick me up and he texts the address of the meeting. I google map it and it's three blocks from where I'm standing. I tell him I'll walk. I get to the meeting and it's a large room with crystals everywhere and soft meditative music playing twenty-four hours a day.

Everyone finally arrives and my friend hands me "How it Works" to read at the beginning of the meeting. He then says, "Welcome to the Over the Rainbow Group of Alcoholics Anonymous!" I start to cry uncontrollably. I can't read. Everybody is looking at me like damn, this guy from Alabama can't read. I finally finish reading it, falteringly.

I notice a girl sitting up front all by herself. They give out sobriety chips at the beginning of the meeting. They ask if anyone has one year of sobriety and the girl up front says, "I do, I do!" Someone yells out "How'd you do it?" She says, "I'm glad you ask," and pulls out a typewritten page out of her back pocket in anticipation of the question being asked. Then she says, "I was on my way to the meeting and I was so filled with gratitude that I haven't taken a drink in a year. I was looking out of the window at the beautiful landscape of Bell Rock when *Somewhere Over the Rainbow* began playing on the radio." I cry some more. Everyone is looking at me with compassion. We go around the room sharing and one guy says, "Oh, April, I'm so proud of you. I remember when we were growing up, I used to call you by your nickname, April Rainbow." I get back from the trip while going through the photographs, I notice a rainbow in one of them. God got my letter.

**The Beginning**

# Acknowledgements

I humbly and gratefully would like to acknowledge and praise my editor, Professor Julie Steward for painstakingly taking this story line by line and giving some suggestions to make the story a little better and more understandable and correct the grammar. Without her help this book would not have been possible as she understood my voice and the importance of keeping the story in its original form. Also, the editors at Friesen Press for showing me the correct punctuation, grammar, and proper stylization's for writing. Also, my Daughter in Law, Emily, who painstakingly re-edited the manuscript and found many corrections to be made! Most editors I talked with told me to take out the crystals and extraterrestrials, however, it is part of my story and later on when I traveled to Southern California, I learned of Howard Menzer, George Van Tassel and the Integratron. A large community gathered in the early nineteen fifties at Giant Rock and watched craft fly around. Both Howard and George communicated with beings from Venus.

I also would like to humbly thank Jonny Enoch for writing the forward to the book. One never knows what impact they have on other people, therefore it is important to be yourself and cause no harm. This intelligence of the Universe, Creator of Worlds chose the perfect people to bring this book into form.

Finally, I would like to thank all my friends, John P., Steve L., Tonya, Eason, Ben and especially Dave A., and many others who have listened to my crazy stories and still love me. (I think)

Please visit my website for pictures and more!

http://thebookofjohn.net

Made in the USA
Middletown, DE
30 October 2022